Clarel by Herman Melville

Part III – (of IV) Mar Saba

Herman Melville was born in New York City on August 1st, 1819, the third of eight children.

At the age of 7 Melville contracted scarlet fever which was to permanently diminish his eyesight. At this time Melville was described as being "very backwards in speech and somewhat slow in comprehension."

His father died when he was 12 leaving the family in very straitened times. Just 14 Melville took a job in a bank paying $150 a year that he obtained via his uncle, Peter Gansevoort, who was one of the directors of the New York State Bank.

After a failed stint as a surveyor he signed on to go to sea and travelled across the Atlantic to Liverpool and then on further voyages to the Pacific on adventures which would soon become the architecture of his novels. Whilst travelling he joined a mutiny, was jailed, fell in love with a South Pacific beauty and became known as a figure of opposition to the coercion of native Hawaiians to the Christian religion.

He drew from these experiences in his books Typee, Omoo, and White-Jacket. These were published as novels, the first initially in London in 1846.

By 1851 his masterpiece, Moby Dick, was ready to be published. It is perhaps, and certainly at the time, one of the most ambitious novels ever written. However, it never sold out its initial print run of 3,000 and Melville's earnings on this masterpiece were a mere $556.37.

In succeeding years his reputation waned and he found life increasingly difficult. His family was growing, now four children, and a stable income was essential.

With his finances in a disappointing state Melville took the advice of friends that a change in career was called for. For many others public lecturing had proved very rewarding. From late 1857 to 1860, Melville embarked upon three lecture tours, where he spoke mainly on Roman statuary and sightseeing in Rome.

In 1876 he was at last able to publish privately his 16,000 line epic poem Clarel. It was to no avail. The book had an initial printing of 350 copies, but sales failed miserably.

On December 31st, 1885 Melville was at last able to retire. His wife had inherited several small legacies and provide them with a reasonable income.

Herman Melville, novelist, poet, short story writer and essayist, died at his home on September 28rh 1891 from cardiovascular disease.

Index of Contents

Canto I - In the Mountain

What reveries be in yonder heaven
Whither, if yet faith rule it so,
The tried and ransomed natures flow?
If there peace after strife be given
Shall hearts remember yet and know?
Thy vista, Lord, of havens dear,
May that in such entrancement bind
That never starts a wandering tear
For wail and willow left behind?

Then wherefore, chaplet, quivering throw
A dusk e'en on the martyr's brow
You crown? Do seraphim shed balm
At last on all of earnest mind,
Unworldly yearners, nor the palm
Awarded St. Teresa, ban
To Leopardi, Obermann?
Translated where the anthem's sung
Beyond the thunder, in a strain
Whose harmony unwinds and solves
Each mystery that life involves;
There shall the Tree whereon He hung,
The olive wood, leaf out again—
Again leaf out, and endless reign,
Type of the peace that buds from sinless pain?

Exhalings! Tending toward the skies
By natural law, from heart they rise
Of one there by the moundless bed
Where stones they roll to feet and head;
Then mount, and fall behind the guard
And so away.
But whitherward?
'Tis the high desert, sultry Alp
Which suns decay, which lightnings scalp.
For now, to round the waste in large,
Christ's Tomb re-win by Saba's marge
Of grots and ossuary cells,
And Bethlehem where remembrance dwells—
From Sodom in her pit dismayed
Westward they wheel, and there invade
Judah's main ridge, which horrors deaden—
Where Chaos holds the wilds in pawn,
As here had happed an Armageddon,
Betwixt the good and ill a fray,
But ending in a battle drawn,
Victory undetermined. Nay,
For how an indecisive day
When one side camps upon the ground
Contested.
Ere, enlocked in bound
They enter where the ridge is riven,
A look, one natural look is given
Toward Margoth and his henchmen twain
Dwindling to ants far off upon the plain.

"So fade men from each other!—Jew,
We do forgive thee now thy scoff,

Now that thou dim recedest off
Forever. Fair hap to thee, Jew:
Consolator whom thou disownest
Attend thee in last hour lonest!"
Rolfe, gazing, could not all repress
That utterance; and more or less,
Albeit they left it undeclared,
The others in the feeling shared.

They turn, and enter now the pass
Wherein, all unredeemed by weeds,
Trees, moss, the winding cornice leads
For road along the calcined mass
Of aged mountain. Slow they urge
Sidelong their way betwixt the wall
And flanked abyss. They hark the fall
Of stones, hoof-loosened, down the crags:
The crumblings note they of the verge.
In rear one strange steed timid lags:
On foot an Arab goes before
And coaxes him to steepy shore
Of scooped-out gulfs, would halt him there:
Back shrinks the foal with snort and glare.
Then downward from the giddy brim
They peep; but hardly may they tell
If the black gulf affrighted him
Or lingering scent he caught in air
From relics in mid lodgment placed,
Now first perceived within the dell—
Two human skeletons inlaced
In grapple as alive they fell,
Or so disposed in overthrow,
As to suggest encounter so.
A ticklish rim, an imminent pass
For quarrel; and blood-feud, alas,
The Arab keeps, and where or when,
Cain meeting Abel, closes then.
That desert's age the gorge may prove,
Piercing profound the mountain bare;
Yet hardly churned out in the groove
By a perennial wear and tear
Of floods; nay, dry it shows within;
But twice a year the waters flow,
Nor then in tide, but dribbling thin:
Avers Mar Saba's abbot so.
Nor less perchance before the day
When Joshua met the tribes in fray,
What wave here ran through leafy scene

Like uplands in Vermont the green;
What sylvan folk by mountain-base
Descrying showers about the crown
Of woods, foreknew the freshet's race
Quick to descend in torrent down
And watched for it, and hailed in glee,
Then rode the comb of freshet wild,
As peaked upon the roller free
With gulls for mates, the Maldives' merry child?
Or, earlier yet, could be a day,
In time's first youth and pristine May
When here the hunter stood alone—
Moccasined Nimrod, belted Boone;
And down the tube of fringed ravine
Siddim descried, a lilied scene?
But crime and earthquake, throes and war;
And heaven remands the flower and star.
Aside they turn, and leave that gorge,
And slant upon the mountain long,
And toward a ledge they toilsome urge
High over Siddim, and overhung
By loftier crags. In spirals curled
And pearly nothings buoyant whirled,
Eddies of exhalations light,
As over lime-kilns, swim in sight.
The fog dispersed, those vapors show
Diurnal from the waters won
By the athirst demanding sun—
Recalling text of Scripture so;
For on the morn which followed rain
Of fire, when Abraham looked again,
The smoke went up from all the plain.
Their mount of vision, voiceless, bare,
It is that ridge, the desert's own,
Which by its dead Medusa stare,
Petrific o'er the valley thrown,
Congeals Arabia into stone.
With dull metallic glint, the sea
Slumbers beneath the silent lee
Of sulphurous hills. These stretch away
Toward wilds of Kadesh Barnea,
And Zin the waste.
In pale regard
Intent the Swede turned thitherward:
"God came from Teman; in His hour
The Holy One from Paran came;
They knew Him not; He hid His power
Within the forking of the flame,

Within the thunder and the roll.
Imperious in its swift control,
The lion's instantaneous lick
Not more effaces to the quick
Than His fierce indignation then.
Look! for His wake is here. O men,
Since Science can so much explode,
Evaporated is this God?—
Recall the red year Forty-eight:
He storms in Paris; thence divides;
The menace scarce outspeeds the fate:
He's over the Rhine He's at Berlin—
At Munich—Dresden—fires Vien;
He's over the Alps—the whirlwind rides
In Rome; London's alert—the Czar:
The portent and the fact of war,
And terror that into hate subsides.
There, through His instruments made known,
Including Atheist and his tribes,
Behold the prophet's marching One,
He at whose coming Midian shook—
The God, the striding God of Habakkuk."

Distempered! Nor might passion tire,
Nor pale reaction from it quell
The craze of grief's intolerant fire
Unwearied and unweariable.

Canto II - The Carpenter

From vehemence too mad to stem
Fain would they turn and solace them.
Turn where they may they find a dart.
For while recumbent here they view,
Beneath them spread, the seats malign,
Nehemiah recurs—in last recline
A hermit there. And some renew
Their wonderment at such a heart,
Single in life—in death, how far apart!
That life they question, seek a clew:
Those virtues which his meekness knew,
Marked these indeed but wreckful wane
Of strength, or the organic man?
The hardy hemlock, if subdued,
Decays to violets in the wood,
Which put forth from the sodden stem:

His virtues, might they breed like them?
Nor less that tale by Rolfe narrated
(Thrown out some theory to achieve),
Erewhile upon Mount Olivet,
That sea-tale of the master fated;
Not wholly might it here receive
An application such as met
The case. It needed something more
Or else, to penetrate the core.
But Clarel—made remindful so
Of by-gone things which death can show
In kindled meaning—here revealed
That once Nehemiah his lips unsealed
(How prompted he could not recall)
In story which seemed rambling all,
And yet, in him, not quite amiss.
In pointed version it was this:
A gentle wight of Jesu's trade,
A carpenter, for years had made
His living in a quiet dell,
And toiled and ate and slept alone,
Esteemed a harmless witless one.
Had I a friend thought he, 'twere well.
A friend he made, and through device
Of jobbing for him without price.
But on a day there came a word—
A word unblest, a blow abhorred.
Thereafter, in the mid of night,
When from the rafter and the joist
The insect ticked; and he, lone sprite,
How wakeful lay, what word was voiced?
Me love; fear only man. And he
He willed what seemed too strange to be:
The hamlet marveled and the glade:
Interring him within his house,
He there his monastery made,
And grew familiar with the mouse.
Down to the beggar who might sing,
Alms, silent alms, unseen he'd fling,
And cakes to children. But no more
Abroad he went, till spent and gray,
Feet foremost he was borne away.

As when upon a misty shore
The watchful seaman marks a light
Blurred by the fog, uncertain quite;
And thereto instant turns the glass
And studies it, and thinks it o'er

By compass: Is't the cape we pass?
So Rolfe from Clarel's mention caught
Food for an eagerness of thought:
"It bears, it bears; such things may be:
Shut from the busy world's pell-mell
And man's aggressive energy—
In cloistral Palestine to dwell
And pace the stone!"
And Mortmain heard,
Attesting; more his look did tell
Than comment of a bitter word.
Meantime the ass, high o'er the bed
Late scooped by Siddim's borders there—
As stupefied by brute despair,
Motionless hung the earthward head.

Canto III - Of the Many Mansions

"The Elysium of the Greek was given
By haughty bards, a hero-heaven;
No victim looked for solace there:
The marble gate disowned the plea—
Ye heavy laden, come to me.
Nor Fortune's Isles, nor Tempe's dale
Nor Araby the Blest did bear
A saving balm—might not avail
To lull one pang, one lot repair.
Dreams, narrow dreams; nor of a kind
Showing inventiveness of mind
Beyond our earth. But oh! 'twas rare,
In world like this, the world we know
(Sole know, and reason from) to dare
To pledge indemnifying good
In worlds not known; boldly avow,
Against experience, the brood
Of Christian hopes."
So Rolfe, and sat
Clouded. But, changing, up he gat:
"Whence sprang the vision? They who freeze,
On earth here, under want or wrong;
The Sermon on the Mount shall these
Find verified? is love so strong?
Or bounds are hers, that Python mars
Your gentler influence, ye stars?
If so, how seem they given o'er
To worse than Circe's fooling spell;

Enslaved, degraded, tractable
To each mean atheist's crafty power.
So winning in enthusiast plea,
Here may the Gospel but the more
Operate like a perfidy?"
"So worldlings deem," the Swede in glow;
"Much so they deem; or, if not so,
Hereon they act. But what said he,
The Jew whose feet the blisters know,
To Christ as sore He trailed the Tree
Toward Golgotha: 'Ha, is it Thou,
The king, the god? Well then, be strong:
No royal steed with galls is wrung:
That's for the hack.' There he but hurled
The scoff of Nature and the World,
Those monstrous twins." It jarred the nerve
Of Derwent, but he masked the thrill.
For Vine, he kindled, sitting still;
Respected he the Swede's wild will
As did the Swede Vine's ruled reserve.
Mortmain went on: "We've touched a theme
From which the club and lyceum swerve,
Nor Herr von Goethe would esteem;
And yet of such compulsive worth,
It dragged a god here down to earth,
As some account. And, truth to say,
Religion oft times, one may deem,
Is man's appeal from fellow-clay:
Thibetan faith implies the extreme—
That death emancipates the good,
Absorbs them into deity,
Dropping the wicked into bestialhood."

With that for text to revery due,
In lifted waste, on ashy ground
Like Job's pale group, without a sound
They sat. But hark! what strains ensue
Voiced from the crags above their view?

Canto IV - The Cypriote

"Noble gods at the board
Where lord unto lord
Light pushes the care-killing wine:
Urbane in their pleasure,
Superb in their leisure—

Lax ease—
Lax ease after labor divine!

"Golden ages eternal,
Autumnal, supernal,
Deep mellow their temper serene:
The rose by their gate
Shall it yield unto fate?
They are gods—
They are gods and their garlands keep green.

"Ever blandly adore them;
But spare to implore them:
They rest, they discharge them from time;
Yet believe, light believe
They would succor, reprieve—
Nay, retrieve—
Might but revelers pause in the prime!"

"Who sings?" cried Rolfe; "dare say no Quaker:
Fine song o'er funeral Siddim here:
So, mindless of the undertaker,
In cage above her mistress' bier
The gold canary chirps. What cheer?
Who comes?"
"Ay, welcome as the drums
Of marching allies unto men
Beleaguered—comes, who hymning comes—
What rescuer, what Delian?"
So Derwent, and with quick remove
Scaling the rock which hemmed their cove
He thence descried where hither yet
A traveler came, by cliffs beset,
Descending, and where terrors met.
Nor Orpheus of heavenly seed
Adown thrilled Hades' gorges singing,
About him personally flinging
The bloom transmitted from the mead;
In listening ghost such thoughts could breed
As did the vocal stranger here
In Mortmain, where relaxed he lay
Under that voice from other sphere
And carol laughing at the clay.
Nearer the minstrel drew. How fair
And light he leaned with easeful air
Backward in saddle, so to frame
A counterpoise as down he came.
Against the dolorous mountain side

His Phrygian cap in scarlet pride
Burned like a cardinal-flower in glen.
And after him, in trappings paced
His escort armed, three goodly men.
Observing now the other train,
He halted. Young he was, and graced
With fortunate aspect, such as draws
Hearts to good-will by natural laws.
No furtive scrutiny he made,
But frankly flung salute, and said:
"Well met in desert! Hear my song?"
"Indeed we did," cried Derwent boon.
"And wondered where you got that tune,"
Rolfe added there. "Oh, brought along
From Cyprus; I'm a Cypriote,
You see; one catches many a note
Wafted from only heaven knows where."
"And, pray, how name you it?" "The air?
Why, hymn of Aristippus." "Ah:
And whither wends your train?" "Not far;"
And sidelong in the saddle free
A thigh he lolled: "'Tis thus, you see:
My dame beneath Our Lady's star
Vowed in her need, to Saba's shrine
Three flagons good for holy wine:
Vowed, and through me performed. Even now
I come from Saba, having done
Her will, accomplishing the vow.
But late I made a private one
Meant to surprise her with a present
She'll value more than juicy pheasant,
Good mother mine. Yes, here I go
To Jordan, in desert there below,
To dip this shroud for her." "Shroud, shroud?"
Cried Derwent, following the hand
In startled wonderment unfeigned,
Which here a little tap bestowed
In designation on a roll
Strapped to the pommel; "Azrael's scroll!
You do not mean you carry there
A—a—" "The same; 'tis woven fair:
"My shroud is saintly linen,
In lavender 'tis laid;
I have chosen a bed by the marigold
And supplied me a silver spade!"

The priest gazed at the singer; then
Turned his perplexed entreating ken

Upon Djalea. But Rolfe explained:
"I chance to know. Last year I gained
The Jordan at the Easter tide,
And saw the Greeks in numbers there,
Men, women, blithe on every side,
Dipping their winding-sheets. With care
They bleach and fold and put away
And take home to await the day:
A custom of old precedent,
And curious too in mode 'tis kept,
Showing how under Christian sway
Greeks still retain their primal bent,
Nor let grave doctrine intercept
That gay Hellene lightheartedness
Which in the pagan years did twine
The funeral urn with fair caress
Of vintage holiday divine."
He turned him toward the Cypriote:
"Your courier, the forerunning note
Which ere we sighted you, we heard—
You're bold to trill it so, my bird."
"And why? It is a fluent song.
Though who they be I cannot say,
I trust their lordships think no wrong;
I do but trill it for the air;
'Tis anything as down we fare."
Enough; Rolfe let him have his way;
Yes, there he let the matter stay.
And so, with mutual good-will shown,
They parted.
           For l'envoy anon
They heard his lilting voice impel
Among the crags this versicle:
"With a rose in thy mouth
Through the world lightly veer:
Rose in the mouth
Makes a rose of the year!"

Then, after interval again,
But fainter, further in the strain:

"With the Prince of the South
O'er the Styx bravely steer:
Rose in the mouth
And a wreath on the bier!"

Chord deeper now that touched within.
Listening, they at each other look;

Some charitable hope they brook,
Yes, vague belief they fondly win
That heaven would brim his happy years
Nor time mature him into tears
And Vine in heart of revery saith:
Like any flute inspired with breath
Pervasive, and which duly renders
Unconscious in melodious play,
Whate'er the light musician tenders;
So warblest thou lay after lay
Scarce self-derived; and (shroud before)
Down goest singing toward Death's Sea,
Where lies aloof our pilgrim hoar
In pit thou'lt pass. Ah, young to be!

Canto V - The High Desert

Where silence and the legend dwell,
A cleft in Horeb is, they tell,
Through which upon one happy day
(The sun on his heraldic track
Due sign having gained in Zodiac)
A sunbeam darts, which slants away
Through ancient carven oriel
Or window in the Convent there,
Illuming so with annual flush
The somber vaulted chamber spare
Of Catherine's Chapel of the Bush—
The Burning Bush. Brief visitant,
It makes no lasting covenant;
It brings, but cannot leave, the ray.
To hearts which here the desert smote
So came, so went the Cypriote.
Derwent deep felt it; and, as fain
His prior spirits to regain;
Impatient too of scenes which led
To converse such as late was bred,
Moved to go on. But some declined.

So, for relief to heart which pined,
Belex he sought, by him sat down
In cordial ease upon a stone
Apart, and heard his stories free
Of Ibrahim's wild infantry.

The rest abide. To these there comes,

As down on Siddim's scene they peer,
The contrast of their vernal homes—
Field, orchard, and the harvest cheer.
At variance in their revery move
The spleen of nature and her love:
At variance, yet entangled too—
Like wrestlers. Here in apt review
They call to mind Abel and Cain—
Ormuzd involved with Ahriman
In deadly lock. Were those gods gone?
Or under other names lived on?
The theme they started. 'Twas averred
That, in old Gnostic pages blurred,
Jehovah was construed to be
Author of evil, yea, its god;
And Christ divine his contrary:
A god was held against a god,
But Christ revered alone. Herefrom,
If inference availeth aught
(For still the topic pressed they home)
The two-fold Testaments become
Transmitters of Chaldaic thought
By implication. If no more
Those Gnostic heretics prevail
Which shook the East from shore to shore,
Their strife forgotten now and pale;
Yet, with the sects, that old revolt
Now reappears, if in assault
Less frank: none say Jehovah's evil,
None gainsay that he bears the rod;
Scarce that; but there's dismission civil,
And Jesus is the indulgent God.

This change, this dusking change that slips
(Like the penumbra o'er the sun),
Over the faith transmitted down;
Foreshadows it complete eclipse?
Science and Faith, can these unite?
Or is that priestly instinct right
(Right as regards conserving still
The Church's reign) whose strenuous will
Made Galileo pale recite
The Penitential Psalms in vest
Of sackcloth; which to-day would blight
Those potent solvents late expressed
In laboratories of the West?
But in her Protestant repose
Snores faith toward her mortal close?

Nay, like a sachem petrified,
Encaved found in the mountain-side,
Perfect in feature, true in limb,
Life's full similitude in him,
Yet all mere stone—is faith dead now,
A petrifaction? Grant it so,
Then what's in store? what shapeless birth?
Reveal the doom reserved for earth?
How far may seas retiring go?
But, to redeem us, shall we say
That faith, undying, does but range,
Casting the skin—the creed. In change
Dead always does some creed delay—
Dead, not interred, though hard upon
Interment's brink? At Saint Denis
Where slept the Capets, sire and son,
Eight centuries of lineal clay,
On steps that led down into vault
The prince inurned last made a halt,
The coffin left they there, 'tis said,
Till the inheritor was dead;
Then, not till then 'twas laid away.
But if no more the creeds be linked,
If the long line's at last extinct,
If time both creed and faith betray,
Vesture and vested—yet again
What interregnum or what reign
Ensues? Or does a period come?
The Sibyl's books lodged in the tomb?
Shall endless time no more unfold
Of truth at core? Some things discerned
By the far Noahs of India old—
Earth's first spectators, the clear-eyed,
Unvitiated, unfalsified
Seers at first hand—shall these be learned
Though late, even by the New World, say,
Which now contemns?
But what shall stay
The fever of advance? London immense
Still wax for aye? A check: but whence?
How of the teeming Prairie-Land?
There shall the plenitude expand
Unthinned, unawed? Or does it need
Only that men should breed and breed
To enrich those forces into play
Which in past times could oversway
Pride at his proudest? Do they come,
The locusts, only to the bloom?

Prosperity sire them?
Thus they swept,
Nor sequence held, consistent tone
Imagination wildering on
Through vacant halls which faith once kept
With ushers good.
Themselves thus lost,
At settled hearts they wonder most.
For those (they asked) who still adhere
In homely habit's dull delay,
To dreams dreamed out or passed away;
Do these, our pagans, all appear
Much like each poor and busy one
Who when the Tartar took Pekin,
(If credence hearsay old may win)
Knew not the fact—so vast the town,
The multitude, the maze, the din?
Still laggeth in deferred adieu
The A. D. (Anno Domini)
Overlapping into era new
Even as the Roman A. U. C.
Yet ran for time, regardless all
That Christ was born, and after fall
Of Rome itself?
But now our age,
So infidel in equipage,
While carrying still the Christian name—
For all its self-asserted claim,
How fares it, tell? Can the age stem
Its own conclusions? is't a king
Awed by his conquests which enring
With menaces his diadem?
Bright visions of the times to be—
Must these recoil, ere long be cowed
Before the march in league avowed
Of Mammon and Democracy?
In one result whereto we tend
Shall Science disappoint the hope,
Yea, to confound us in the end,
New doors to superstition ope?
As years, as years and annals grow,
And action and reaction vie,
And never men attain, but know
How waves on waves forever die;
Does all more enigmatic show?

So they; and in the vain appeal
Persisted yet, as ever still

Blown back in sleet that blinds the eyes,
Not less the fervid Geysers rise.

Clarel meantime ungladdened bent
Regardful, and the more intent
For silence held. At whiles his eye
Lit on the Druze, reclined half prone,
The long pipe resting on the stone
And wreaths of vapor floating by—
The man and pipe in peace as one.
How clear the profile, clear and true;
And he so tawny. Bust ye view,
Antique, in alabaster brown,
Might show like that. There, all aside,
How passionless he took for bride
The calm—the calm, but not the dearth—
The dearth or waste; nor would he fall
In waste of words, that waste of all.

For Vine, from that unchristened earth
Bits he picked up of porous stone,
And crushed in fist: or one by one,
Through the dull void of desert air,
He tossed them into valley down;
Or pelted his own shadow there;
Nor sided he with anything:
By fits, indeed, he wakeful looked;
But, in the main, how ill he brooked
That weary length of arguing—
Like tale interminable told
In Hades by some gossip old
To while the never-ending night.

Apart he went. Meantime, like kite
On Sidon perched, which doth enfold,
Slowly exact, the noiseless wing:
Each wrinkled Arab Bethlehemite,
Or trooper of the Arab ring,
With look of Endor's withered sprite
Slant peered on them from lateral hight;
While unperturbed over deserts riven,
Stretched the clear vault of hollow heaven.

Canto VI – Derwent

At night upon the darkling main

To ship return with muffled sound
The rowers without comment vain—
The messmate overboard not found:
So, baffled in deep quest but late,
These on the mountain.
But from chat
With Belex in campaigning mood,
Derwent drew nigh. The sight of him
Ruffled the Swede- choked a whim
Which took these words: "O, well bestowed!
Hither and help us, man of God:
Doctor of consolation, here!
Be warned though: truth won't docile be
To codes of good society."
Allowing for pain's bitter jeer,
Or hearing but in part perchance,
The comely cleric pilgrim came
With what he might of suiting frame,
And air approaching nonchalance;
And "How to serve you, friends?" he said.
"Ah, that!" cried Rolfe; "for we, misled,
We peer from brinks of all we know;
Our eyes are blurred against the haze:
Canst help us track in snow on snow
The footprint of the Ancient of Days?"
"Scarce without snow-shoes;" Derwent mild
In gravity; "But come; we've whiled
The time; up then, and let us go."
"Delay," said Mortmain; "stay, roseace:
What word is thine for sinking heart,
What is thy wont in such a case,
Who sends for thee to act thy part
Consoling—not in life's last hour
Indeed—but when some deprivation sore
Unnerves, and every hope lies flat?"
That troubled Derwent, for the tone
Brake into tremble unbeknown
E'en to the speaker. Down he sat
Beside them: "Well, if such one—nay!
But never yet such sent for me—
I mean, none in that last degree;
Assume it though: to him I'd say—
'The less in hand the more in store,
Dear friend.' No formula I'd trace,
But honest comfort face to face;
And, yes, with tonic strong I'd brace,
Closing with cheerful Paul in lore
Of text—Rejoice ye evermore. "

The Swede here of a sudden drooped,
A hump dropped on him, one would say;
He reached and some burnt gravel scooped,
Then stared down on the plain away.
The priest in fidget moved to part.
"Abide," said Mortmain with a start;
"Abide, for more I yet would know:
Is God an omnipresent God?
Is He in Siddim yonder? No?
If anywhere He's disavowed
How think to shun the final schism—
Blind elements, flat atheism?"
Whereto the priest: "Far let it be
That ground where Durham's prelate stood
Who saw no proof that God was good
But only righteous.—Woe is me!
These controversies. Oft I've said
That never, never would I be led
Into their maze of vanity.
Behead me—rid me of pride's part
And let me live but by the heart!"
"Hast proved thy heart? first prove it. Stay:
The Bible, tell me, is it true,
And thence deriv'st thy flattering view?"
But Derwent glanced aside, as vexed;
Inly assured, nor less perplexed
How to impart; and grieved too late
At being drawn within the strait
Of vexed discussion: nor quite free
From ill conjecture, that the Swede,
Though no dissembler, yet indeed
Part played on him: "Why question me?
Why pound the text? Ah, modern be,
And share the truth's munificence.
Look now, one reasons thus: Immense
Is tropic India; hence she breeds
Brahma tremendous, gods like seeds.
The genial clime of Hellas gay
Begat Apollo. Take that way;
Nor query—Ramayana true?
The Iliad?"
Mortmain nothing said,
But lumped his limbs and sunk his head.
Then Rolfe to Derwent: "But the Jew:
Since clime and country, as you own,
So much effect, how with the Jew
Herein?"
There Derwent sat him down

Afresh, well pleased and leisurely,
As one in favorite theory
Invoked: "That bondman from his doom
By Nile, and subsequent distress,
With punishment in wilderness,
Methinks he brought an added gloom
To nature here. Here church and state
He founded—would perpetuate
Exclusive and withdrawn. But no:
Advancing years prohibit rest;
All turns or alters for the best.
Time ran; and that expansive light
Of Greeks about the bordering sea,
Their happy genial spirits bright,
Wit, grace urbane, amenity
Contagious, and so hard to ban
By bigot law, or any plan;
These influences stole their way,
Affecting here and there a Jew;
Likewise the Magi tincture too
Derived from the Captivity:
Hence Hillel's fair reforming school,
Liberal gloss and leavening rule.
How then? could other issue be
At last but ferment and a change?
True, none recanted or dared range:
To Moses' law they yet did cling,
But some would fain have tempering—
In the bare place a bit of green.
And lo, an advent—the Essene,
Gentle and holy, meek, retired,
With virgin charity inspired:
Precursor, nay, a pledge, agree,
Of light to break from Galilee.
And, ay, He comes: the lilies blow!
In hamlet, field, and on the road,
To every man, in every mode
How did the crowning Teacher show
His broad and blessed comity.
I do avow He still doth seem
Pontiff of optimists supreme!"
The Swede sat stone-like. Suddenly:
"Leave thy carmine! From thorns the streak
Ruddies enough that tortured cheek.
'Twas Shaftesbury first assumed your tone,
Trying to cheerfulize Christ's moan."
"Nay now," plead Derwent, earnest here,
And in his eyes the forming tear;

"But hear me, hear!"
"No more of it!"
And rose. It was his passion-fit.
The other changed; his pleasant cheer,
Confronted by that aspect wild,
Dropped like the flower from Ceres' child
In Enna, seeing the pale brow
Of Pluto dank from scud below.

Though by Gethsemane, where first
Derwent encountered Mortmain's mien.

Christian forbearance well he nursed,
Allowing for distempered spleen;
Now all was altered, quite reversed—
'Twas now as at the burial scene
By Siddim's marge. And yet—and yet
Was here a proof that priest had met
His confutation? Hardly so
(Mused Clarel) but he longed to know
How it could be, that while the rest
Contented scarce the splenetic Swede,
They hardly so provoked the man
To biting outburst unrepressed
As did the cleric's gentle fan.
But had the student paid more heed
To Derwent's look, he might have caught
Hints of reserves within the thought.
Nor failed the priest ere all too late
His patience here to vindicate.

Canto VII - Bell and Cairn

"ELOI LAMA SABACHTHANI!"
And, swooning, strove no more.
Nor gone
For every heart, whate'er they say,
The eclipse that cry of cries brought down,
And clamors through the darkness blown.
More wide for some it spreads in sway,
Involves the lily of the Easter Day.

A chance word of the Swede in place—
Allusion to the anguished face,
Recalled to Clarel now the cry,
The ghost's reproachful litany.

Disturbed then, he apart would go;
And passed among the crags; and there,
Like David in Adullam's lair—
Could it be Vine, and quivering so?

'Twas Vine. He wore that nameless look
About the mouth—so hard to brook—
Which in the Cenci portrait shows,
Lost in each copy, oil or print;
Lost, or else slurred, as 'twere a hint
Which if received, few might sustain:
A trembling over of small throes
In weak swoll'n lips, which to restrain
Desire is none, nor any rein.
Clarel recalled the garden's shade,
And Vine therein, with all that made
The estrangement in Gethsemane.
Reserves laid bare? and can it be?
The dock-yard forge's silent mound,
Played over by small nimble flame—
Raked open, lo, the anchor's found
In white-heat's alb.
With shrinking frame,
Grateful that he was unespied,
Clarel quite noiseless slipped aside:
Ill hour (thought he), an evil sign:
No more need dream of winning Vine
Or coming at his mystery.
O, lives which languish in the shade,
Puzzle and tease us, or upbraid;
What noteless confidant, may be,

Withholds the talisman, the key!
Or if indeed it run not so,
And he's above me where I cling;
Then how these higher natures know
Except in shadow from the wing.—
Hark! as in benison to all,
Borne on waste air in wasteful clime,
What swell on swell of mellowing chime,
Which every drooping pilgrim rallies;
How much unlike that ominous call
Pealed in the blast from Roncesvalles!
Was more than silver in this shell
By distance toned. What festival?
What feast? of Adam's kind, or fay?
Hark—no, not yet it dies away.
Where the sexton of the vaulted seas

Buries the drowned in weedy grave,
While tolls the buoy-bell down the breeze;
There, off the shoals of rainy wave
Outside the channel which they crave,
The sailors lost in shrouding mist,
Unto that muffled knelling list,
The more because for fogged remove
The floating belfry none may prove;
So, yet with difference, do these
Attend.
    "Chimes, chimes? but whence? thou breeze;"
Here Derwent; "convent none is near."
"Ay," said the Druze, "but quick's the ear
In deep hush of the desert wide."
"'Tis Saba calling; yea," Rolfe cried,
"Saba, Mar Saba summons us:
O, hither, pilgrims, turn to me,
Escape the desert perilous;
Here's refuge, hither unto me!"

A lateral lodgment won, they wheeled,
And toward the abandoned ledge they glanced:
Near, in the high void waste advanced,
They saw, in turn abrupt revealed,
An object reared aloof by Vine
In whim of silence, when debate
Was held upon the cliff but late
And ended where all words decline:
A heap of stones in arid state.

The cairn (thought Clarel), meant he—yes,
A monument to barrenness?

Canto VIII - Tents of Kedar

They climb. In Indian file they gain
A sheeted blank white lifted plain—
A moor of chalk, or slimy clay,
With gluey track and streaky trail
Of some small slug or torpid snail.
With hooded brows against the sun,
Man after man they labor on.
Corrupt and mortally intense,
What fumes ere long pollute the sense?
But, hark the flap and lumbering rise
Of launching wing; see the gaunt size

Of the ground-shadow thereby thrown.
Behind a great and sheltering stone
A camel, worn out, down had laid—
Never to rise. 'Tis thence the kite
Ascends, sails off in Tyreward flight.
As 'twere Apollyon, angel bad,
They watch him as he speeds away.
But Vine, in mere caprice of clay,
Or else because a pride had birth
Slighting high claims which vaunted be
And favoring things of low degree
From heaven he turned him down to earth,
Eagle to ass. She now, ahead
Went riderless, with even tread
And in official manner, sooth,
For bell and cord she'd known in youth;
Through mart and wild, bazaar and waste
Preceding camels strung in train,
Full often had the dwarf thing paced,
Conductress of the caravan
Of creatures tall. What meant Vine's glance
Ironic here which impish ran
In thievish way? O, world's advance:
We wise limp after!
                    The cavalcade
Anon file by a pit-like glade
Clean scooped of last lean dregs of soil;
Attesting in rude terraced stones
The ancient husbandmen's hard toil,—
All now a valley of dry bones—
In shape a hopper. 'Twas a sight
So marked with dead, dead undelight,
That Derwent half unconscious here
Stole a quick glance at Mortmain's face
To note how it received the cheer.
Whereat the moody man, with sting
Returned the imprudent glance apace—
Wayward retort all withering
Though wordless. Clarel looking on,
Saw there repeated the wild tone
Of that discountenancing late
In sequel to prolonged debate
Upon the mountain. And again
Puzzled, and earnest, less to know
What rasped the Swede in such a man
Than how indeed the priest could show
Such strange forbearance; ventured now
To put a question to him fair.

"Oh, oh," he answered, all his air
Recovered from the disarray;
"The shadow flung by Ebal's hill
On Gerizim, it cannot stay,
But passes. Ay, and ever still—
But don't you see the man is mad?
His fits he has; sad, sad, how sad!
Besides; but let me tell you now;
Do you read Greek? Well, long ago,
In stage when goslings try the wing,
And peacock-chicks would softly sing,
And roosters small essay to crow;
Reading Theocritus divine,
Envious I grew of all that charm
Where sweet and simple so entwine;
But I plucked up and won a balm:
Thought I, I'll beat him in his place:
If, in my verses, and what not,
If I can't have this pagan grace,
Still—nor alone in page I blot,
But all encounters that may be
I'll make it up with Christian charity."

Another brink they win, and view
Adown in faintly greenish hollow
An oval camp of sable hue
Pitched full across the track they follow—
Twelve tents of shaggy goat's wool dun.
"Ah, tents of Kedar may these be,"
Cried Derwent; "named by Solomon
In song? Black, but scarce comely, see.
Whom have we here? The brood of Lot?"
"The oval seems his burial-plot,"
Said Rolfe; "and, for his brood, these men—
They rove perchance from Moab's den
Or Ammon's. Belex here seems well
To know them, and no doubt will tell."
The Spahi, not at all remiss
In airing his Turk prejudice,
Exclaimed: "Ay, sirs; and ill betide
These Moabites and Ammonites
Ferrying Jordan either side—
Robbers and starvelings, mangy wights.

Sirs, I will vouch one thing they do:
Each year they harry Jericho
In harvest; yet thereby they gain
But meager, rusty spears of grain.

What right have such black thieves to live?
Much more to think here to receive
Our toll? Just Allah! say the word,
And " here he signified with sword
The rest, impatient of delay
While yet on hight at brink they stay,
So bidden by Djalea, who slow
Descends into the hopper low,
Riding. "To parley with the knaves!"
Cried Belex; "spur them down; that saves
All trouble, sirs; 'twas Ibrahim's way;
When, in the Lebanon one day
We came upon a "
"Pardon me,
The priest; "but look how leisurely
He enters; yes, and straight he goes
To meet our friend with scowling brows,
The warder in yon outlet, see,
Holding his desert spear transverse,
Bar-like, from sable hearse to hearse
Of toll-gate tents. Foreboding ill,
The woman calls there to her brood.
But what's to fear! Ah, with good-will
They bustle in the war-like mood;
Save us from those long fish-pole lances!
Look, menacingly one advances;
But he, our Druze, he mindeth none,
But paces. So! they soften down.
'Tis Zar, it is that dainty steed,
High-bred fine equine lady brave,
Of stock derived from long ago;
'Tis she they now admiring heed,
Picking her mincing way so grave,
None jostling, grazing scarce a toe
Of all the press. The sulky clan,
Yes, make way for the mare—and man!
There's homage!"
"Ay, ay," Belex said,
"They'd like to steal her and retire:
Her beauty is their heart's desire—
Base jackals with their jades! "
Well sped
The Druze. The champion he nears
Posted in outlet, keeping ward,
Who, altering at that aspect, peers,
And him needs own for natural lord.
Though claiming kingship of the land
He hesitates to make demand:

Salute he yields. The Druze returns
The salutation; nor he spurns
To smoke with Ammon, but in way
Not derogating—brief delay.
They part. The unmolested train
Are beckoned, and come down. Amain
The camp they enter and pass through;
No conflict here, no weak ado
Of words or blows.
This policy
(Djalea's) bred now a pleasing thought
In Derwent: "Wars might ended be,
Yes, Japhet, Shem, and Ham be brought
To confluence of amity,
Were leaders but discreet and wise
Like this our chief."
The armed man's eyes
Turned toward him tolerantly there
As 'twere a prattling child.
They fare
Further, and win a nook of stone,
And there a fountain making moan.
The shade invites, though not of trees:
They tarry in this chapel-of-ease;
Then up, and journey on and on,
Nor tent they see—not even a lonely one.

Canto IX - Of Monasteries

The lake ink-black mid slopes of snow—
The dead-house for the frozen, barred—
And the stone hospice; chill they show
Monastic in thy pass, Bernard.
Apostle of the Alps storm-riven,
How lone didst build so near the heaven!
Anchored in seas of Nitria's sand,
The desert convent of the Copt—
No aerolite can more command

The sense of dead detachment, dropped
All solitary from the sky.
The herdsmen of Olympus lie
In summer when the eve is won
Viewing white Spermos lower down,
The mountain-convent; and winds bear
The chimes that bid the monks to prayer;

Nor man-of-war-hawk sole in sky
O'er lonely ship sends lonelier cry.
The Grand Chartreuse with crystal peaks
Mid pines—the wintry Paradise
Of soul which but a Saviour seeks—
The mountains round all slabbed with ice;
May well recall the founder true,
St. Bruno, who to heaven has gone
And proved his motto—that whereto
Each locked Carthusian yet adheres:
Troubled I was, but spake I none;
I kept in mind the eternal years.
And Vallambrosa—in, shut in;
And Montserrat—enisled aloft;
With many more the verse might win,
Solitudes all, austere or soft.

But Saba! Of retreats where heart
Longing for more than downy rest,
Fit place would find from world apart,
Saba abides the loneliest:
Saba, that with an eagle's theft
Seizeth and dwelleth in the cleft.
Aloof the monks their aerie keep,
Down from their hanging cells they peep
Like samphire-gatherers o'er the bay
Faint hearing there the hammering deep
Of surf that smites the ledges gray.

But up and down, from grot to shrine,
Along the gorge, hard by the brink
File the gowned monks in even line,
And never shrink!
With litany or dirge they wend
Where nature as in travail dwells;
And the worn grots and pensive dells
In wail for wail responses send—
Echoes in plaintive syllables.
With mystic silvery brede divine,
Saint Basil's banner of Our Lord
(In lieu of crucifix adored
BY Greeks which images decline)
Stained with the five small wounds and red,
Down through the darkling gulf is led—
BY night oft times, while tapers glow
Small in the depths, as stars may show
Reflected far in well profound.

Full fifteen hundred years have wound
Since cenobite first harbored here;
The bones of men, deemed martyrs crowned,
To fossils turn in mountain near;
Nor less while now lone scribe may write,
Even now, in living dead of night,
In Saba's lamps the flames aspire—
The votaries tend the far-transmitted fire.

Canto X - Before the Gate

'Tis Kedron, that profound ravine
Whence Saba soars. And all between
Zion and Saba one may stray,
Sunk from the sun, through Kedron's way.
BY road more menacingly dead
Than that which wins the convent's base
No ghost to Tartarus is led.
Through scuttle small, that keepeth place
In floor of cellars which impend—
Cellars or cloisters—men ascend
BY ladder which the monks let down
And quick withdraw; and thence yet on
Higher and higher, flight by flight,
They mount from Erebus to light,
And off look, world-wide, much in tone
Of Uriel, warder in the sun,
Who serious views this earthly scene
Since Satan passed his guard and entered in.
But not by Kedron these now come
Who ride from Siddim; no, they roam
The roof of mountains—win the tall
Towers of Saba, and huge wall
Builded along the steep, and there
A postern with a door, full spare
Yet strong, a clamped and bucklered mass
Bolted. In waste whose king is Fear,
Sole port of refuge, it is here.
Strange (and it might repel, alas)
Fair haven's won by such a pass.
In London Tower the Traitors' Gate
Through which the guilty waters flow,
Looks not more grim. Yet shalt thou know,
If once thou enter, good estate.
Beneath these walls what frays have been,
What clash and outery, sabers crossed

Pilgrim and Perizzite between;
And some have here given up the ghost
Before the gate in last despair.
Nor, for the most part, lacking fair
Sign-manual from a mitered lord,
Admission shall that arch afford
To any.
Weary now the train
At eve halt by the gate and knock.
No answer. Belex shouts amain:
As well invoke the Pico Rock.
"Bide," breathes the Druze, and dropping rein,
He points. A wallet's lowered down
From under where a hood projects
High up the tower, a cowl of stone,
Wherefrom alert an eye inspects
All applicants, and unbeknown.
Djalea promptly from his vest
A missive draws, which duly placed
In budget, rises from the ground
And vanishes. So, without sound
Monks fish up to their donjon dark
The voucher from their Patriarch,
Even him who dwells in damask state
On Zion throned. Not long they wait:
The postern swings. Dismounting nigh,
The horses through the needle's eye,
That small and narrow gate, they lead.
But while low ducks each lofty steed,
Behold how through the crucial pass
Slips unabased the humble ass.
And so they all with clattering din
The stony fortress court-yard win.
There see them served, and bidden rest;
Horse, ass too, treated as a guest.
Friars tend as grooms. Yet others call
And lead them to the frater-hall
Cliff-hung. By monks the board is spread;
They break the monastery bread,
Moist'ning the same with Saba's wine,
Product of painful toil mid stones
In terraces, whose Bacchic zones
That desert gird. Olive and vine
To flinty places well incline,
Once crush the flint. Even so they fared,
So well for them the brethren cared.
Refection done, for grateful bed
Cool mats of dye sedate, were spread:

The lamps were looked to, freshly trimmed;
And last (at hint from mellow man
Who seemed to know how all things ran,
And who in place shall soon be hymned)
A young monk-servant, slender-limbed,
And of a comely countenance,
Set out one flask of stature tall,
Against men's needs medicinal,
Travelers, subject to mischance;
Devout then, and with aspect bright
Invoked Mar Saba's blessing—bade good night.

He goes. But now in change of tune,
Shall friar be followed by buffoon?
Saba supply a Pantaloon?
Wise largess of true license yield.
Howe'er the river, winding round,
May win an unexpected bound;
The aim and destiny, unsealed
In the first fount, hold unrepealed.

Canto XI - The Beaker

"Life is not by square and line:
Wisdom's stupid without folly:
Sherbet to-day, to-morrow wine
Feather in cap and the world is jolly!"

So he, the aforesaid mellow man,
Thrumming upon the table's span.
Scarce audible except in air
Mirth's modest overture seemed there.
Nor less the pilgrims, folding wing,
Weary, would now in slumber fall—
Sleep, held for a superfluous thing
By that free heart at home in hall.
And who was he so jovial?
Purveyor, he some needful stores
Supplied from Syrian towns and shores;
And on his trips, dismissing care,—
His stores delivered all and told,
Would rest awhile in Saba's fold.
Not broken he with fast and prayer:
The leg did well plump out the sock;
Nor young, nor old, but did enlock
In reconcilement a bright cheek

And fleecy beard; that cheek, in show,
Arbutus flaked about with snow,
Running-arbutus in Spring's freak
Overtaken so. In Mytilene,
Sappho and Phaon's Lesbos green,
His home was, his lax Paradise,
An island yet luxurious seen,
Fruitful in all that can entice.
For chum he had a mountaineer,
A giant man, beneath whose lee
Lightly he bloomed, like pinks that cheer
The base of tower where cannon be.
That mountaineer the battle tans,
An Arnaut of no mean degree,
A lion of war, and drew descent
Through dames heroic, from the tent
Of Pyrrhus and those Epirot clans
Which routed Rome. And, furthermore,
In after-line enlinked he stood
To Scanderbeg's Albanian brood,
And Arslan, famous heretofore,
The horse-tail pennon dyed in gore.
An Islamite he was by creed—
In act, what fortune's chances breed:
Attest the medal, vouch the scar—
Had bled for Sultan, won for Czar;
His psalter bugle was and drum,
Any scorched rag his Labarum.
For time adherent of the Turk,
In Saba's hold he sheathed his dirk,
Waiting arrival of a troop
Destined for some dragooning swoop
On the wild tribes beyond the wave
Of Jordan. Unconstrained though grave,
Stalwart but agile, nobly tall,
Complexion a burnt red, and all
His carriage charged with courage high
And devil-dare. A hawk's his eye.
While, for the garb: a snow-white kilt
Was background to his great sword-hilt:
The waistcoat blue, with plates and chains
Tarnished a bit with grapy stains;
Oaches in silver rows: stout greaves
Of leather: buskins thonged; light cloak
Of broidered stuff Damascus weaves;
And, scorched one side with powder smoke,
A crimson Fez, bald as a skull
Save for long tassel prodigal.

Last, add hereto a blood-red sash,
With dagger and pistol's silvery charms,
And there you have this Arnaut rash,
In zone of war—a trophy of arms.
While yet the monks stood by serene,
He as to kill time, his moustache
Adjusted in his scimeter's sheen;
But when they made their mild adieu,
Response he nodded, seemly too.
And now, the last gowned friar gone,
His heart of onslaught he toned down
Into a solemn sort of grace,
Each pilgrim looking full in face,
As he should say: Why now, let's be
Good comrades here to-night.
Grave plea
For brotherly love and jollity
From such an arsenal of man,
A little strange seemed and remote.
To bring it nearer—spice—promote—
Nor mindless of some aspects wan,
Lesbos, with fair engaging tone,
Threw in some moral cinnamon:
"Sir pilgrims, look; 'tis early yet;
In evening arbor here forget
The heat, the burden of the day.
Life has its trials, sorrows—yes,
I know—I feel; but blessedness
Makes up. Ye've grieved the tender clay:
Solace should now all that requite;
'Tis duty, sirs. And—by the way—
Not vainly Anselm bade good night,
For see!" and cheery on the board
The flask he set.
"I and the sword"
The Arnaut said (and in a tone
Of natural bass which startled onc
Profound as the profound trombone)
"I and the sword stand by the red.
But this will pass, this molten ore
Of yellow gold. Is there no more?"
"Trust wit for that," the other said:
"Purveyor, shall he not purvey?"
And slid a panel, showing store
Of cups and bottles in array.
"Then arms at ease, and ho, the bench!"
It made the slender student blench
To hark the jangling of the steel,

Vibration of the floor to feel,
Tremor through beams and bones which ran
As that ripe masterpiece of man
Plumped solid down upon the deal.

Derwent a little hung behind—
Censorious not, nor disinclined,
But with self-querying countenance,
As if one of the cloth, perchance
Due bound should set, observe degree
In liberal play of social glee.
Through instinct of good fellow bright
His poise, as seemed, the Lesbian wight
Divined: and justly deeming here
The stage required a riper cheer
Than that before—solicitous,
With bubbling cup in either hand,
Toward Derwent drew he, archly bland;
Then posed; and tunefully e'en thus:
"A shady rock, and trickling too,
Is good to meet in desert drear:
Prithee now, the beading here
Beads of Saba, saintly dew:
Quaffit, sweetheart, I and you:
Quaff it, for thereby ye bless
Beadsmen here in wilderness.
Spite of sorrow, maugre sin,
Bless their larder and laud their bin:
Nor deem that here they vainly pine
Who toil for heaven and till the vine!"

He sings; and in the act of singing,
Near and more near one cup he's bringing,
Till by his genial sleight of hand
'Tis lodged in Derwent's, and—retained.
As lit by vintage sunset's hue
Which mellow warms the grapes that bleed,
In amber light the good man view;
Nor text of sanction lacked at need;
"At Cana, who renewed the wine?
Sourly did I this cup decline
(Which lo, I quaff, and not for food),
'Twould by an implication rude
Asperse that festival benign.—
We're brethren, ay!"
The lamps disclose
The Spahi, Arnaut, and the priest,
With Rolfe and the not-of-Sharon Rose,

Ranged at the board for family feast.
"But where's Djalea?" the cleric cried;
"'Tis royalty should here preside:"
And looked about him. Truth to own,
The Druze, his office having done
And brought them into haven there,
Discharged himself of further care
Till the next start: the interim
Accounting rightfully his own;
And may be, heedful not to dim
The escutcheon of an Emir's son
By any needless letting down.

The Lesbian who had Derwent served,
Officiated for them all;
And, as from man to man he swerved,
Grotesque a bit of song let fall:
"The Mufti in park suburban
Lies under a stone
Surmounted serene by a turban
Magnific—a marble one!"

So, man by man, with twinkling air,
And cup and text of stanza fair:
"A Rabbi in Prague they muster
In mound evermore
Looking up at his monument's cluster—
A cluster of grapes of Noah!"

When all were served with wine and rhyme
"Ho, comrade," cried armed Og sublime,
"Your singing makes the filling scant;
The flask to me, let me decant."
With that, the host he played—brimmed up
And off-hand pushed the frequent cup;
Flung out his thigh, and quaffed apace,
Barbaric in his hardy grace;
The while his haughty port did say,
Who 's here uncivilized, I pray?
I know good customs: stint I ye?
Indeed (thought Rolfe), a man of mark,
And makes a rare symposiarch;
I like him; I'll e'en feel his grip.

With that, in vinous fellowship
Frank he put out his hand. In mood
Of questionable brotherhood
The slayer stared—anon construed

The overture aright, and yet
Not unreservedly he met
The palm. Came it in sort too close?
Was it embraces were for foes?

Rolfe, noting a fine color stir
Flushing each happy reveler,
Now leaned back, with this ditty wee:
"The Mountain-Ash
And Sumach fine,
Tipplers of summer,
Betray the wine
In autumn leaf
Of vermil flame:
Bramble and Thorn
Cry—Fie, for shame!"

Mortmain aloof and single sat—
In range with Rolfe, as viewed from mat
Where Vine reposed, observing there
That these in contour of the head
And goodly profile made a pair,
Though one looked like a statue dead.
Methinks (mused Vine), 'tis Ahab's court
And yon the Tishbite; he'll consort
Not long, but Kedron seek. It proved
Even so: the desert-heart removed.
But he of bins, whose wakeful eye
On him had fixed, and followed sly
Until the shadow left the door,
Turned short, and tristful visage wore
In quaint appeal. A shrug; and then
"Beseech ye now, ye friendly men,
Who's he—a cup, pray;—O, my faith!

That funeral cap of his means death
To all good fellowship in feast.
Mad, say he's mad!"
Awhile the priest
And Rolfe, reminded here in heart
Of more than well they might impart,
Uneasy sat. But this went by:
Ill sort some truths with revelry.—
The giant plied the flask. For Vine,
Relaxed he viewed nor spurned the wine,
But humorously moralized
On those five souls imparadised
For term how brief; well pleased to scan

The Mytilene, the juicy man.
Earth—of the earth (thought Vine) well, well,
So's a fresh turf, but good the smell,
Yes, deemed by some medicinal—
Most too if damped with wine of Xeres
And snuffed at when the spirit wearies.
I have it under strong advising
'Tis good at whiles this sensualizing;
Would I could joy in it myself;
But no!—
For Derwent, he, light elf,
Not vainly stifling recent fret,
Under the table his two knees
Pushed deeper, so as e'en to get
Closer in comradeship at ease.
Arnaut and Spahi, in respect
Of all adventures they had known,
These chiefly did the priest affect:
Adventures, such as duly shown
Printed in books, seem passing strange
To clerks which read them by the fire,
Yet be the wonted common-place
Of some who in the Orient range,
Free-lances, spendthrifts of their hire,
And who in end, when they retrace
Their lives, see little to admire
Or wonder at, so dull they be
(Like fish mid marvels of the sea)
To every thing that is not pent
In self, or thereto ministrant.

Canto XII - The Timoneer's Story

But ere those Sinbads had begun
Their Orient Decameron,
Rolfe rose, to view the further hall.
Here showed, set up against the wall,
Heroic traditionary arms,
Protecting tutelary charms
(Like Godfrey's sword and Baldwin's spur
In treasury of the Sepulcher,
Wherewith they knighthood yet confer,
The monks or their Superior)
Sanctified heirlooms of old time;
With trophies of the Paynim clime;
These last with tarnish on the gilt,

And jewels vanished from the hilt.
Upon one serpent-curving blade
Love-motto beamed from Antar's rhyme
In Arabic. A second said
(A scimiter the Turk had made,
And likely, it had clove a skull)
IN NAME OF GOD THE MERCIFUL!
A third was given suspended place,
And as in salutation waved,
And in old Greek was finely graved
With this: HAIL, MARY, FULL OF GRACE!

'Tis a rare sheaf of arms be here,
Thought Rolfe: "Who's this?" and turned to peer
At one who had but late come in,
(A stranger) and, avoiding din
Made by each distant reveler,
Anchored beside him. His sea-gear
Announced a pilgrim-timoneer.
The weird and weather-beaten face,
Bearded and pitted, and fine vexed
With wrinkles of cabala text,
Did yet reveal a twinge-like trace
Of some late trial undergone:
Nor less a beauty grave pertained
To him, part such as is ordained
I'o Eld, for each age hath its own,
And even scars may share the tone.
Bald was his head as any bell—
Quite bald, except a silvery round
Of small curled bud-like locks which bound
His temples as with asphodel.
Such he, who in nigh nook disturbed
Upon his mat by late uncurbed
Light revel, came with air subdued,
And by the clustered arms here stood
Regarding them with dullish eye
Of some old reminiscence sad.
On him Rolfe gazed: "And do ye sigh?
Hardly they seem to cheer ye: why?"
He pursed the mouth and shook the head.
"But speak!" "'Tis but an old bewailing."
"No matter, tell." "'Twere unavailing."
"Come, now."

"Since you entreat of me
'Tis long ago—I'm aged, see:
From Egypt sailing—hurrying too—

For spite the sky there, always blue,
And blue daubed seas so bland, the pest
Was breaking out—the people quailing
In houses hushed; from Egypt sailing,
In ship, I say, which shunned the pest,
Cargo half-stored, and—and—alack!
One passenger of visage black,
But whom a white robe did invest
And linen turban, like the rest—
A Moor he was, with but a chest;—
A fugitive poor Wahabee—
So ran his story—who by me
Was smuggled aboard; and ah, a crew
That did their wrangles still renew,
Jabbing the poignard in the fray,
And mutinous withal;—I say,
From Egypt bound for Venice sailing—
On Friday—well might heart forebode!
In this same craft from Cadiz hailing,
Christened by friar 'The Peace of God, '
(She laden now with rusted cannon
Which long beneath the Crescent's pennon
On beach had laid, condemned and dead,
Beneath a rampart, and from bed
Were shipped off to be sold and smelted
And into new artillery melted)
I say that to The Peace of God
(Your iron the salt seas corrode)
I say there fell to her unblest
A hap more baleful than the pest.
Yea, from the first I knew a fear,
So strangely did the needle veer.
A gale came up, with frequent din
Of cracking thunder out and in:
Corposants on yard-arms did burn,
Red lightning forked upon the stern:
The needle like an imp did spin.
Three gulls continual plied in wake,
Which wriggled like a wounded snake,
For I, the wretched timoneer,
By fitful stars yet tried to steer
'Neath shortened sail. The needle flew
(The glass thick blurred with damp and dew),
And flew the ship we knew not where.
Meantime the mutinous bad crew
Got at the casks and drowned despair,
Carousing, fighting. What to do?
To all the saints I put up prayer,

Seeing against the gloomy shades
Breakers in ghastly palisades.
Nevertheless she took the rocks;
And dinning through the grinds and shocks,
(Attend the solving of the riddle)
I heard the clattering of blades
Shaken within the Moor's strong box
In cabin underneath the needle.
How screamed those three birds round the mast
Slant going over. The keel was broken
And heaved aboard us for death-token.
To quit the wreck I was the last,
Yet I sole wight that 'scaped the sea."
"But he, the Moor?"
"O, sorcery!
For him no heaven is, no atoner.
He proved an armorer, theJonah!
And dealt in blades that poisoned were,
A black lieutenant of Lucifer.
I heard in Algiers, as befell
Afterward, his crimes of hell.
I'm far from superstitious, see;
But arms in sheaf, somehow they trouble me."

"Ha, trouble, trouble? what's that, pray?
I've heard of it; bad thing, they say;
"Bug there, lady bug, plumped in your wine?
Only rose-leaves flutter by mine!"

The gracioso man, 'twas he,
Flagon in hand, held tiltingly.
How peered at him that timoneer,
With what a changed, still, merman-cheer,
As much he could, but would not say:
So murmuring naught, he moved away.
"Old, old," the Lesbian dropped; "old—dry:
Remainder biscuit; and alas,
But recent 'scaped from luckless pass."
"Indeed? relate."—"O, by-and-by."

But Rolfe would have it then. And so
The incident narrated was
Forthwith.
Re-cast, it thus may flow:
The ship men of the Cyclades
Being Greeks, even of St. Saba's creed,
Are frequent pilgrims. From the seas
Greek convents welcome them, and feed.

Agath, with hardy messmates ten,
To Saba, and on foot, had fared
From Joppa. Duly in the Glen
His prayers he said; but rashly dared
Afar to range without the wall.
Upon him fell a robber-brood,
Some Ammonites. Choking his call,
They beat and stripped him, drawing blood,
And left him prone. His mates made search
With friars, and ere night found him so,
And bore him moaning back to porch
Of Saba's refuge. Cure proved slow;
The end his messmates might not wait;
Therefore they left him unto love
And charity—within that gate
Not lacking. Mended now in main,
Or convalescent, he would fain
Back unto Joppa make remove
With the first charitable train.
His story told, the teller turned
And seemed like one who instant yearned
To rid him of intrusive sigh:
"Yon happier pilgrim, by-the-by—
I like him: his vocation, pray?
Purveyor he? like me, purvey?"
"Ay—for the conscience: he's our priest."
"Priest? he's a grape, judicious one
Keeps on the right side of the sun.
But here's a song I heard at feast."

Canto XIII - Song and Recitative

"The chalice tall of beaten gold
Is hung with bells about:
The flamen serves in temple old,
And weirdly are the tinklings rolled
When he pours libation out.
O Cybele, dread Cybele,
Thy turrets nod, thy terrors be!

"But service done, and vestment doffed,
With cronies in a row
Behind night's violet velvet soft,
The chalice drained he rings aloft
To another tune, I trow.
O Cybele, fine Cybele,

Jolly thy bins and belfries be!"

With action timing well the song,
His flagon flourished up in air,
The varlet of the isle so flung
His mad-cap intimation—there
Comic on Rolfe his eye retaining
In mirth how full of roguish feigning.
Ought I protest? (thought Rolfe) the man
Nor malice has, nor faith: why ban
This heart though of religion scant,
A true child of the lax Levant,
That polyglot and loose-laced mother?
In such variety he's lived
Where creeds dovetail into each other;
Such influences he's received:
Thrown among all—Medes, Elamites,
Egyptians, Jews and proselytes,
Strangers from Rome, and men of Crete—
And parts of Lybia round Cyrenc
Arabians, and the throngs ye meet
On Smyrna's quays, and all between
Stamboul and Fez:—thrown among these,
A caterer to revelries,
He's caught the tints of many a scene,
And so become a harlequin
Gay patchwork of all levities.
Holding to now, swearing by here,
His course conducting by no keen
Observance of the stellar sphere—
He coasteth under sail latteen:
Then let him laugh, enjoy his dinner,
He's an excusable poor sinner.
'Twas Rolfe. But Clarel, what thought he?
For he too heard the Lesbian's song
There by the casement where he hung:
In heart of Saba's mystery
This mocker light!—
But now in waltz
The Pantaloon here Rolfe assaults;
Then, keeping arm around his waist,
Sees Rolfe's reciprocally placed;
'Tis side-by-side entwined in ease
Of Chang and Eng the Siamese
When leaning mutually embraced;
And so these improvised twin brothers
Dance forward and salute the others,
The Lesbian flourishing for sign

His wine-cup, though it lacked the wine.
They sit. With random scraps of song
He whips the tandem hours along,
Or moments, rather; in the end
Calling on Derwent to unbend
In lyric.
"I?" said Derwent, "I?
Well, if you like, I'll even give
A trifle in recitative—
A something—nothing—anything—
Since little does it signify
In festive free contributing:
"To Hafiz in grape-arbor comes
Didymus, with book he thumbs:
My lord Hafiz, priest of bowers—
Flowers in such a world as ours?
Who is the god of all these flowers?—
"Signior Didymus, who knows?
None the less I take repose—
Believe, and worship here with wine
In vaulted chapel of the vine
Before the altar of the rose.

"Ah, who sits here? a sailor meek?"
It was that sea-appareled Greek.
"Gray brother, here, partake our wine."
He shook his head, yes, did decline.
"Or quaff or sing," cried Derwent then,
"For learn, we be hilarious men.
Pray, now, you seamen know to sing."
"I'm old," he breathed.—"So's many a tree,
Yet green the leaves and dance in glee."
The Arnaut made the scabbard ring:
"Sing, man, and here's the chorus—sing!"
"Sing, sing!" the Islesman, "bear the bell;
Sing, and the other songs excel."
"Ay, sing," cried Rolfe, "here now's a sample;
'Tis virtue teaches by example:
'Jars of honey,
Wine-skin, dates, and macaroni:
Falling back upon the senses—
O, the wrong—
Need take up with recompenses:
Song, a song!"

They sang about him till he said:
"Sing, sirs, I cannot: this I'll do,
Repeat a thing Methodius made,

Good chaplain of The Apostles' crew:
"Priest in ship with saintly bow,
War-ship named from Paul and Peter
Grandly carved on castled prow;
Gliding by the grouped Canaries
Under liquid light of Mary's
Mellow star of eventide;
Lulled by tinklings at the side,
I, along the taffrail leaning,
Yielding to the ship's careening,
Shared that peace the upland owns
Where the palm—the palm and pine
Meeting on the frontier line
Seal a truce between the zones.
This be ever! (mused I lowly)
Dear repose is this and holy;
Like the Gospel it is gracious
And prevailing.—There, audacious—
Boom! the signal-gun it jarred me,
Flash and boom together marred me,
And I thought of horrid war;
But never moved grand Paul and Peter,
Never blenched Our Lady's star!"

Canto XIV - The Revel Closed

"Bless that good chaplain," Derwent here;
"All doves and halcyons round the sphere
Defend him from war's rude alarms!"
Then (Oh, sweet impudence of wine)
Then rising and approaching Vine
In suppliant way: "I crave an alms:
Since this gray guest, this serious one,
Our wrinkled old Euroclydon,
Since even he, with genial breath
His quota here contributeth,
Helping our gladness to prolong—
Thou too! Nay, nay; as everywhere
Water is found if one not spare
To delve tale, prithee now, or song!"
Vine's brow shot up with crimson lights
As may the North on frosty nights
Over Dilston Hall and his low state
The fair young Earl whose bloody end
Those red rays do commemorate,
And take his name.

Now all did bend
In chorus, crying, "Tale or song!"
Investing him. Was no escape
Beset by such a Bacchic throng.
"Ambushed in leaves we spy your grape,"
Cried Derwent; "black but juicy one
A song!"
No way for Vine to shun:
"Well, if you'll let me here recline
At ease the while, I'll hum a word
Which in his Florence loft I heard
An artist trill one morning fine:—
"What is beauty? 'tis a dream
Dispensing still with gladness:
The dolphin haunteth not the shoal,
And deeps there be in sadness.

"The rose-leaves, see, disbanded be
Blowing, about me blowing;
But on the death-bed of the rose
My amaranths are growing.

"His amaranths: a fond conceit,
Yes, last illusion of retreat!
Short measure 'tis." "And yet enough,"
Said Derwent; "'tis a hopeful song;
Or, if part sad, not less adorning,
Like purple in a royal mourning.
We debtors be. Now come along
To table, we'll take no rebuff."
So Vine sat down among them then—
Adept—shy prying into men.
Derwent here wheeled him: "But for sake
Of conscience, noble Arnaut, tell;
When now I as from dream awake
It just dawns on me: how is this?
Wine-bibbing? No! that kind of bliss
Your Koran bars. And Belex, man,
Thou'st smoked before the sun low fell;
And this month's what? your Ramadan?
May true believers thus rebel?"
Good sooth, did neither know to tell,
Or care to know, what time did fall
The Islam fast; yet took it so
As Derwent roguish prompted, though
It was no Ramadan at all;
'Twas far ahead, a movable fast
Of lunar month, which to forecast

Needs reckoning.
Ponderous pause
The Anak made: "Mahone has laws,
And Allah's great—of course:—forefend!
Ho, rouse a stave, and so an end:
"The Bey, the Emir, and Mamalook lords
Charged down on the field in a grove of swords:
Hurrah! hurrah and hurrah
For the grove of swords in the wind of war!

"And the Bey to the Emir exclaimed, Who knows?
In the shade of the scimiters Paradise shows!
Hurrah! hurrah and hurrah
For the grove of swords in the wind of war!"

He sang; then settled down, a mate
For Mars' high pontiff—solemn sate,
And on his long broad Bazra blade
Deep ruminated. Less sedate,
The Spahi now in escapade
Vented some Turkish guard-room joke,
But scarce thereby the other woke
To laughter, for he never laughed,
Into whatever mood he broke,
Nor verbal levity vouchsafed,
So leonine the man. But here
The Spahi, with another cheer
Into a vein of mockery ran,
Toasting the feast of Ramadan,
Laughing thereat, removed from fear.
It was a deep-mouthed mastiff burst,
Nor less, for all the jovial tone
The echo startling import won—
At least for Clarel, little versed
In men, their levities and tides
Unequal, and of much besides.
There by a lattice open swung
Over the Kedron's gulf he hung,
And pored and pondered: With what sweep
Doubt plunges, and from maw to maw;
Traditions none the nations keep—
Old ties dissolve in one wide thaw;
The Frank, the Turk, and e'en the Jew
Share it; perchance the Brahmin too.
Returns each thing that may withdraw?
The schools of blue-fish years desert
Our sounds and shores—but they revert;
The ship returns on her long tack:

The bones of Theseus are brought back:
A comet shall resume its path
Though three millenniums go. But faith?
Ah, Nehemiah—and, Derwent, thou!
'Twas dust to dust: what is it now
And here? Is life indeed a dream?
Are these the pilgrims late that heard
The wheeling desert vultures scream
Above the Man and Book interred—
Scream like the haglet and the gull
Off Chiloe o'er the foundered hull?

But hark: while here light fell the clink
The five cups made touched brink to brink
In fair bouquet of fellowship,
And just as the gay Lesbian's lip
Was parted—jetting came a wail
In litany from Kedron's jail
Profound, and belly of the whale:
"Lord, have mercy.
Christ, have mercy.
Intercedefor me,
Angel of the Agony.
Spare me, spare me!
Merciful be—
Lord, spare me—
Spare and deliver me!"

Arrested, those five revelers there,
Fixed in light postures of their glee,
Seemed problematic shapes ye see
In linked caprice of festal air
Graved round the Greek sarcophagi.

Canto XV - In Moonlight

The roller upon Borneo's strand
Halts not, but in recoiling throe
Drags back the shells involved with sand,
Shuffled and muffled in the flow
And hollow of the wallowing undertow.

In night Rolfe waked, and whelming felt
That refluence of disquiet dealt
In sequel to redundant joy.
Around he gazed in vague annoy

Upon his mates. The lamp-light dim
Obscurely showed them, strangely thrown
In sleep, nor heeding eye of him;
Flung every way, with random limb—
Like corses, when the battle's done
And stars come up. No sound but slight
Calm breathing, or low elfin shriek
In dream. But Mortmain, coiled in plight,
Lay with one arm wedged under cheek,
Mumbling by starts the other hand,
As the wolf-hound the bone. Rolfe rose
And shook him. Whereat, from his throes
He started, glaring; then lapsed down:
"Soft, soft and tender; feels so bland—
Grind it! 'tis hers, Brinvilliers' hand,
My nurse." From which mad dream anon
He seemed his frame to re-command;
And yet would give an animal moan.
"God help thee, and may such ice make
Except against some solid? nay—
But thou who mark'st, get thee away,
Nor in such coals of Tartarus rake."
So Rolfe; and wide a casement threw.
Aroma! and is this Judaea?
Down the long gorge of Kedron blew
A balm beyond the sweet Sabaea—
An air as from Elysian grass;
Such freshening redolence divine
As mariners upon the brine
Inhale, when barren beach they pass
By night; a musk of wafted spoil
From Nature's scent-bags in the soil,
Not in her flowers; nor seems it known
Even on the shores wherefrom 'tis blown.
Clarel, he likewise wakeful grew,
And rose, joined Rolfe, and both repaired
Out to a railed-in ledge. In view
Across the gulf a fox was scared
Even by their quiet coming so,
And noiseless fled along a line
Of giddy cornice, till more slow
He skulked out of the clear moonshine;
For great part of that wall did show,
To these beneath the shadowed hight,
With arras hung of fair moon-light.

The lime-stone mountain cloven asunder,
With scars of many a plunge and shock

Tremendous of the rifted rock;
So hushed now after all the thunder,
Begat a pain of troubled wonder.
The student felt it; for redress
He turned him—anywhere to find
Some simple thing to ease the mind
Dejected in her littleness.
Rolfe read him; and in quiet way
Would interpose, lead off, allay.
"Look," whispered he, "yon object white—
This side here, on the crag at brink—
'Tis touched, just touched by paler light;
Stood we in Finland, one might think
An ermine there lay coiled. But no,
A turban 'tis, Djalea's, aloof
Reclining, as he used to do
In Lebanon upon proud roof—
His sire's. And, see, long pipe in state,
He inhales the friendly fume sedate.
Yon turban with the snowy folds
Announces that my lord there holds
The rank of Druze initiate—
Not versed in portion mere, but total—
Advanced in secrets sacerdotal;
Though what these be, or high or low,
Who dreams? Might Lady Esther learn?"
"Who?"
"Lady Esther. Don't you know?
Pitt's sibyl-niece, who made sojourn
In Libanus, and read the stars;
Self-exiled lady, long ago
She prophesied of wizard wars,
And kept a saddled steed in stall
Awaiting some Messiah's call
Who came not.—But yon Druze's veil
Of Sais may one lift, nor quail?
We'll try."

To courteous challenge sent,
The Druze responded, not by word
Indeed, but act: he came; content
He leaned beside them in accord,
Resting the pipe-bowl. His assent
In joining them, nay, all his air
Mute testimony seemed to bear
That now night's siren element,
Stealing upon his inner frame,
Pliant had made it and more tame.

With welcome having greeted him,
Rolfe led along by easy skim
And won the topic: "Tell us here—
Your Druze faith: are there not degrees,
Orders, ascents of mysteries
Therein? One would not pry and peer:
Of course there's no disclosing these;
But what's that working thought you win?
The prelate-princes of your kin,
They—they—doubtless they take their ease."
No ripple stirred the Emir's son,
He whiffed the vapor, kept him staid,
Then from the lip the amber won:
"No God there is but God," he said,
And tapped the ashes from the bowl,
And stood. 'Twas passive self-control
Of Pallas' statue in sacked Rome
Which bode till pushed from off the plinth;
Then through the rocky labyrinth
Betook him where cool sleep might come;
But not before farewell sedate:—
"Allah preserve ye, Allah great!"

Canto XVI - The Easter Fire

"There's politesse! we're left behind.
And yet I like this Prince of Pith;
Too pithy almost. Where'll ye find
Nobleman to keep silence with
Better than Lord Djalea.?—But you—
It can not be this interview
Has somehow—" "No," said Clarel; "no,
And sighed; then, "How irreverent
Was Belex in the wassail-flow:
His Ramadan he links with Lent."
"No marvel: what else to infer?
Toll-taker at the Sepulcher.
To me he gave his history late,
The which I sought.—You've marked the state
Of warders shawled, on old divan,
Sword, pipe, and coffee-cup at knee,
Cross-legg'd within that portal's span
Which wins the Holy Tomb? Ay me,
With what a bored dead apathy
Faith's eager pilgrims they let in!"
"Guard of the Urn has Belex been?"

Said Clarel, starting; "why then,—yes—"
He checked himself.—
"Nay, but confess,"
Cried Rolfe; "I know the revery lurks:
Frankly admit that for these Turks
There's nothing that can so entice
To disbelieve, nay, Atheize-
Nothing so baneful unto them
As shrined El Cods, Jerusalem.
For look now how it operates:
To Christ the Turk as much as Frank
Concedes a supernatural rank;
Our Holy Places too he mates
All but with Mecca's own. But then
If chance he mark the Cross profaned
By violence of Christian men
So called—his faith then needs be strained;
The more, if he himself have done
(Enforced thereto by harsh command)
Irreverence unto Mary's Son."
"How mean you?" and the speaker scanned.
"Why not alone has Belex been
An idling guard about The Tomb:
Nay, but he knows another scene
In fray beneath the self-same dome
At festivals. What backs he's scored
When on the day by Greeks adored,
St. Basil's Easter, all the friars
Schismatic, with the pilgrim tribes,
Levantine, Russian, heave their tides
Of uproar in among the shrines,
Waiting the burst of fraudful fires
From vent there in the Holy Tomb
Which closeteth the mongers. Room!
It jets! To quell the rush, the lines
Of soldiers sway: crack falls the thong;
And mid the press, some there, though strong,
Are trampled, trodden, till they die.
In transfer swift, igniting fly
The magic flames, which, caught along
By countless candles, multiply.
Like seas phosphoric on calm nights,
Blue shows the fane in fog of lights;
But here 'tis hurricane and high:
Zeal, furious zeal, and frenzying faith
And ecstasy of Atys' scath
When up the Phrygian mount he rushed
Bleeding, yet heeding not his shame,

While round him frantic timbrels pushed
In rites delirious to name.
No: Dindymus' nor Brahma's crew
Dream what these Christian fakirs do:
Wrecked banners, crosses, ragged palms—
Red wounds thro' vestments white ye view;
And priests who shout ferocious psalms
And hoarse hosannas to their king,
Even Christ; and naught may work a lull,
Nor timely truce of reason bring;
Not cutting lash, nor smiting sword,
Nor yet—Oh! more than wonderful—
The tomb, the pleading tomb where lay Our Lord."
"But who ordains the imposture? speak."
"The vivid, ever-inventive Greek."
"The Greek? But that is hard to think.
Seemly the port, gentle the cheer
Of friars which lodge upon this brink
Of Kedron, and do worship here
With rites august, and keep the creed."—
"Ah, rites august;—this ancient sect,
Stately upholstered and bedecked,
Is but a catafalque, concede
Prolongs in sacerdotal way
The Lower Empire's bastard sway;
It does not grow, it does but bide
An orthodoxy petrified.
Or, if it grow, it grows but with
Russia, and thence derives its pith.
The Czar is its armed bishop. See,
The Czar's purse, so it comes to me,
Contributes to this convent's pride.
But what's that twinkling through the gloom
Far down? the lights in chantry? Yes!
Whence came the flame that lit? Confess,
E'en from Jerusalem—the Tomb,
Last Easter. Horseman from the porch
Hither each Easter spurs with torch
To re-ignite the flames extinct
Upon Good-Friday. Thus, you see,
Contagious is this cheatery;
Nay, that's unhandsome; guests we are;
And hosts are sacred—house and all;
And one may think, and scarcely mar
The truth, that it may so befall
That, as yon docile lamps receive
The fraudful flame, yet honest burn,
So, no collusive guile may cleave

Unto these simple friars, who turn
And take whate'er the forms dispense,
Nor question, Wherefore? ask not, Whence? "

Clarel, as if in search of aught
To mitigate unwelcome thought,
Appealed to turret, crag and star;
But all was strange, withdrawn and far.

"Yet need we grant," Rolfe here resumed,
"This trick its source had in a dream
Artless, which few will disesteem—
That angels verily illumed
Those lamps at Easter, long ago;
Though now indeed all come from prayer
(As Greeks believe at least avow)
Of bishops in the Sepulcher.
Be rumor just, which small birds sing,
Greek churchmen would let drop this thing
Of fraud, e'en let it cease. But no:
'Tis ancient, 'tis entangled so
With vital things of needful sway,
Scarce dare they deviate that way.
The Latin in this spurious rite
Joined with the Greek: but long ago,
Long years since, he abjured it quite.
Still, few Rome's pilgrims here, and they
Less credulous than Greeks to-day.
Now worldlings in their worldliness
Enjoin upon us, Never retract:
With ignorant folk, think you, no less
Of policy priesteraft may exact?
But Luther's clergy: though their deeds
Take not imposture, yet 'tis seen
That, in some matters more abstract,
These, too, may be impeached herein.
While, as each plain observer heeds,
Some doctrines fall away from creeds,
And therewith, hopes, which scarce again,
In those same forms, shall solace men—

Perchance, suspended and inert
May hang, with few to controvert,
For ages; does the Lutheran,
To such disciples as may sit
Receptive of his sanctioned wit,
In candor own the dubious weather
And lengthen out the cable's tether?—

You catch my drift?"
"I do. But, nay,
Some ease the cable."
"Derwent, pray?
Ah, he—he is a generous wight,
And lets it slip, yes, run out quite.
Whether now in his priestly state
He seek indeed to mediate
'Tween faith and science (which still slight
Each truce deceptive) or discreet
Would kindly cover faith's retreat,
Alike he labors vainly. Nay,
And, since I think it, why not say—
Things all diverse he would unite:
His idol's an hermaphrodite."
The student shrank. Again he knew
Return for Rolfe of quick distaste;
But mastered it; for still the hue
Rolfe kept of candor undefaced,
Quoting pure nature at his need,
As 'twere the Venerable Bede:
An Adam in his natural ways.
But scrupulous lest any phrase
Through inference might seem unjust
Unto the friend they here discussed
Rolfe supplements: "Derwent but errs—
No, buoyantly but overstates
In much his genial heart avers:
I cannot dream he simulates.
For pulpiteers which make their mart—
Who, in the Truth not for a day,
Debarred from growth as from decay,
Truth one forever, Scriptures say,
Do yet the fine progressive part
So jauntily maintain; these find
(For sciolists abound) a kind
And favoring audience. But none
Exceed in flushed repute the one
Who bold can harmonize for all
Moses and Comte, Renan and Paul:
'Tis the robustious circus-man:
With legs astride the dappled span
Elate he drives white, black, before:
The small apprentices adore.
Astute ones be though, staid and grave
Who in the wars of Faith and Science
Remind one of old tactics brave
Imposing front of false defiance:

The King a corpse in armor led
On a live horse.—You turn your head:
You hardly like that. Woe is me:
What would you have? For one to hold
That he must still trim down, and cold
Dissemble this were coxcombry!
Indulgence should with frankness mate:
Fraternal be: Ah, tolerate!"
The modulated voice here won
Ingress where scarce the plea alone
Had entrance gained. But—to forget
Allusions which no welcome met
In him who heard—Rolfe thus went on:
"Never I've seen it; but they claim
That the Greek prelate's artifice
Comes as a tragic after-piece
To farce, or rather prank and game;
Racers and tumblers round the Tomb:
Sports such as might the mound confront,
The funeral mound, by Hellespont,
Of slain Patroclus. Linger still
Such games beneath some groves of bloom
In mid Pacific, where life's thrill
Is primal—Pagan; and fauns deck
Green theatres for that tattooed Greek
The Polynesian.—Who will say
These Syrians are more wise than they,
Or more humane? not those, believe,
Who may the narrative receive
Of Ibrahim the conqueror, borne
Dead-faint, by soldiers red with gore
Over slippery corses heaped forlorn
Out from splashed Calvary through the door
Into heaven's light. Urged to ordain
That nevermore the frenzying ray
Should issue—'That would but sustain
The cry of persecution; nay,
Let Allah, if he will, remand
These sects to reason. Let it stand.'—
Cynical Moslem! but didst err,
Arch-Captain of the Sepulcher?"—

He stayed: and Clarel knew decline
Of all his spirits, as may one
Who hears some story of his line
Which shows him half his house undone.
Revulsion came: with lifted brows
He gazed on Rolfe: Is this the man

Whom Jordan heard in part espouse
The appeal of that Dominican
And Rome? and here, all sects, behold
All creeds involving in one fold
Of doubt? Better a partisan!
Earnest he seems: can union be
'Twixt earnestness and levity?
Or need at last in Rolfe confess
Thy hollow, Many sidedness!

But, timely, here diversion fell.
Dawn broke; and from each cliff-hung cell
'Twas hailed with hymns—confusion sweet
As of some aviary's seat:
Commemorative matin din:
'Tis Saba's festival they usher in.

Canto XVII - A Chant

That day, though to the convent brood
A holiday, was kept in mood
Of serious sort, yet took the tone
And livery of legend grown
Poetical if grave. The fane
Was garnished, and it heard a strain
Reserved for festa. And befell
That now and then at interval
Some, gathered on the cliffs around,
Would sing Saint Cosmas' canticle;
Some read aloud from book embrowned
While others listened; some prefer
A chant in Scripture character,
Or monkish sort of melodrame.

Upon one group the pilgrims came
In gallery of slender space,
Locked in the echoing embrace
Of crags: a choir of seemly men
Reposed in cirque, nor wanting grace,

Whose tones went eddying down the glen:

First Voice
No more the princes flout the word—
Jeremiah's in dungeon cast:
The siege is up, the walls give way:

This desolation is the last.
The Chaldee army, pouring in,
Fiercer grown for disarray,
Hunt Zedekiah that fleeth out:
Baal and Assyria win:
Israel's last king is shamed in rout,
Taken and blinded, chains put on,
And captive dragged to Babylon.

Second Voice
O daughter of Jerusalem,
Cast up the ashes on the brow!
Nergal and Samgar, Sarsechim
Break down thy towers, abase thee now.

Third Voice
Oh, now each lover leaveth!

Fourth Voice
None comfort me, she saith:

First Voice
Abroad the sword bereaveth:

Second Voice
At home there is as death.

The Four
Behold, behold! the days foretold begin:
A sword without—the pestilence within.

First and Second Voices
But thou that pull'st the city down,
Ah, vauntest thou thy glory so?

Second and Third Voices
God is against thee, haughty one;
His archers roundabout thee go:

The Four
Earth shall be moved, the nations groan
At the jar of Bel and Babylon
In din of overthrow.

First Voice
But Zion shall be built again!

Third and Fourth Voices

Nor shepherd from the flock shall sever;
For lo, his mercy doth remain,
His tender mercy—

Second Voice
And forever!

The Four
Forever and forever!

Choral
Forever and forever
His mercy shall remain:
In rivers flow forever,
Forever fall in rain!

Canto XVIII - The Minister

Huge be the buttresses enmassed
Which shoulder up, like Titan men,
Against the precipices vast
The ancient minster of the glen.

One holds the library four-square,
A study, but with students few:
Books, manuscripts, and—cobwebs too.
Within, the church were rich and rare
But for the time-stain which ye see:
Gilded with venerable gold,
It shows in magnified degree
Much like some tarnished casket old
Which in the dusty place ye view
Through window of the broker Jew.
But Asiatic pomp adheres
To ministry and ministers
Of Basil's Church; that night 'twas seen
In all that festival confers:
Plate of Byzantium, stones and spars,
Urim and Thummim, gold and green;
Music like cymbals clashed in wars
Of great Semiramis the queen.
And texts sonorous they intone
From parchment, not plebeian print;
From old and golden parchment brown
They voice the old Septuagint,
And Gospels, and Epistles, all

Jn the same tongue employed by Paul.
Flags, beatific flags they view:
Ascetics which the hair-cloth knew
And wooden pillow, here were seen
Pictured on satin soft—serene
In fair translation. But advanced
Above the others, and enhanced
About the staff with ring and boss,
They mark the standard of the Cross.
That emblem, here, in Eastern form,
For Derwent seemed to have a charm.
"I like this Greek cross, it has grace;"
He whispered Rolfe: "the Greeks eschew
The long limb; beauty must have place—
Attic! I like it. And do you?"
"Better I'd like it, were it true."
"What mean you there?"

"I do but mean
'Tis not the cross of Calvary's scene.
The Latin cross (by that name known)
Holds the true semblance; that's the one
Was lifted up and knew the nail;
'Tis realistic—can avail!"
Breathed Derwent then, "These arches quite
Set off and aggrandize the rite:
A goodly fane. The incense, though,
Somehow it drugs, makes sleepy so.
They purpose down there in ravine
Having an auto, act, or scene,
Or something. Come, pray, let us go."

Canto XIX - The Masque

'Tis night, with silence, save low moan
Of winds. By torches red in glen
A muffled man upon a stone
Sits desolate sole denizen.
Pilgrims and friars on ledge above
Repose. A figure in remove
This prologue renders: "He in view
Is that Cartaphilus, the Jew
Who wanders ever; in low state,
Behold him in Jehoshaphat
The valley, underneath the hem
And towers of gray Jerusalem:

This must ye feign. With quick conceit
Ingenuous, attuned in heart,
Help out the actor in his part,
And gracious be;" and made retreat.
Then slouching rose the muffled man;
Gazed toward the turrets, and began:
"O city yonder,
Exposed in penalty and wonder,
Again thou seest me! Hither I
Still drawn am by the guilty tie
Between us; all the load I bear
Only thou know'st, for thou dost share.
As round my heart the phantoms throng
Of tribe and era perished long,
So thou art haunted, sister in wrong!
While ghosts from mounds of recent date
Invest and knock at every gatc
Specters of thirty sieges old
Your outer line of trenches hold:
Egyptian, Mede, Greek, Arab, Turk,
Roman, and Frank, beleaguering lurk.—
"Jerusalem!
Not solely for that bond of doom
Between us, do I frequent come
Hither, and make profound resort
In Shaveh's dale, in Joel's court;
But hungering also for the day
Whose dawn these weary feet shall stay,
When Michael's trump the call shall spread
Through all your warrens of the dead.
"Time, never may I know the calm
Till then? my lull the world's alarm?
But many mortal fears and feelings
In me, in me here stand reversed:
The unappeased judicial pealings
Wrench me, not wither me, accursed.
'Just let him live, just let him rove,'
(Pronounced the voice estranged from love)
'Live—live and rove the sea and land,'
Long live, rove far, and understand
And sum all knowledge for his dower;
For he forbid is, he is banned;
His brain shall tingle, but his hand
Shall palsied be in power:
Ruthless, he meriteth no ruth,
On him I imprecate the truth.' "

He quailed; then, after little truce,

Moaned querulous:
"My fate!
Cut off I am, made separate;
For man's embrace I strive no more;
For, would I be
Friendly with one, the mystery
He guesses of that dreadful lore
Which Eld accumulates in me:
He fleeth me.
My face begetteth superstition:
In dungeons of Spain's Inquisition
Thrice languished I for sorcery,
An Elymas. In Venice, long
Immured beneath the wave I lay
For a conspirator. Some wrong
On me is heaped, go where I may,
Among mankind. Hence solitude
Elect I; in waste places brood
More lonely than an only god;
For, human still, I yearn, I yearn,
Yea, after a millennium, turn
Back to my wife, my wife and boy;
Yet ever I shun the dear abode
Or site thereof, of homely joy.
I fold ye in the watch of night,
Esther! then start. And hast thou been?
And I for ages in this plight?
Caitiff I am; but there's no sin
Conjecturable, possible,
No crime they expiate in hell
Justly whereto such pangs belong:
The wrongdoer he endureth wrong.
Yea, now the Jew, inhuman erst,
With penal sympathy is cursed—
The burden shares of every crime,
And throttled miseries undirged,
Unchronicled, and guilt submerged
Each moment in the flood of time.
Go mad I can not: I maintain
The perilous outpost of the sane.
Memory could I mitigate,
Or would the long years vary any!
But no, 'tis fate repeating fate:
Banquet and war, bridal and hate,
And tumults of the people many;
And wind, and dust soon laid again:
Vanity, vanity's endless reign!—
What's there?"

He paused, and all was hush
Save a wild screech, and hurtling rush
Of wings. An owl—the hermit true
Of grot the eremite once knew
Up in the cleft—alarmed by ray
Of shifted flambeau, burst from cave
On bushy wing, and brushed away
Down the long Kedron gorge and grave.

"It flees, but it will be at rest
Anon! But I—" and hung oppressed—
"Years, three-score years, seem much to men;
Three hundred—five—eight hundred, then;
And add a thousand; these I know!
That eighth dim cycle of my woe,
The which, ahead, did so delay,
To me now seems but yesterday:
To Rome I wandered out of Spain,
And saw thy crowning, Charlemagne,
On Christmas eve. Is all but dream?
Or is this Shaveh, and on high,
Is that, even that, Jerusalem?—
How long, how long? Compute hereby:
The years, the penal years to be,
Reckon by years, years, years, and years
Whose calendar thou here mayst see
On grave-slabs which the blister sears—
Of ancient Jews which sought this clime,
Inscriptions nigh extinct,
Or blent or interlinked
With dotard scrawl of idiot Time.
Transported felon on the seas
Pacing the deck while spray-clouds freeze;
Pacing and pacing, night and morn,
Until he staggers overworn;
Through time, so I, Christ's convict grim,
Deathless and sleepless lurching fare
Deathless and sleepless through remorse for Him;
Deathless, when sleepless were enough to bear."

Rising he slouched along the glen,
Halting at base of crag—detached
Erect, as from the barrier snatched,
And upright lodged below; and then:
"Absalom's Pillar! See the shoal
Before it—pebble, flint, and stone,
With malediction, jeer or groan
Cast through long ages. Ah, what soul

That was but human, without sin,
Did hither the first just missile spin!
Culprit am I—this hand flings none;
Rather through yon dark-yawning gap,
Missed by the rabble in mishap
Of peltings vain—abject I'd go,
And, contrite, coil down there within,
Lie still, and try to ease the throe.
"But nay—away!
Not long the feet unblest may stay.
They come: the vengeful vixens strive-
The harpies, lo—hag, gorgon, drive!"

There caught along, as swept by sand
In fierce Sahara hurricaned,
He fled, and vanished down the glen.

The Spahi, who absorbed had been
By the true acting, turned amain,
And letting go the mental strain,
Vented a resonant, "Bismillah!"
Strange answering which pealed from on high—
"Dies irae, dies illa!"
They looked, and through the lurid fume
Profuse of torches that but die,
And ghastly there the cliffs illume;
The skull-capped man they mark on high—
Fitful revealed, as when, through rift
Of clouds which dyed by sunset drift,
The Matterhorn shows its cragged austerity.

Canto XX - Afterward

"Seedsmen of old Saturn's land,
Love and peace went hand in hand,
And sowed the Era Golden!

"Golden time for man and mead:
Title none, nor title-deed,
Nor any slave, nor Soldan.

"Venus burned both large and bright,
Honey-moon from night to night,
Nor bride, nor groom waxed olden.

"Big the tears, but ruddy ones,

Crushed from grapes in vats and tuns
Of vineyards green and golden!

"Sweet to sour did never sue,
None repented ardor true—
Those years did so embolden.

"Glum Don Grave airs slunk in den:
Frankly roved the gods with men
In gracious talk and golden.

"Thrill it, cymbals of my rhyme,
Power was love, and love in prime,
Nor revel to toil beholden.

"Back, come back, good age, and reign,
Goodly age, and long remain—
Saturnian Age, the Golden!"

The masquer gone, by stairs that climb,
In seemly sort, the friars withdrew;
And, waiting that, the Islesman threw
His couplets of the Arcadian time,
Then turning on the pilgrims: "Hoo!
"The bird of Paradise don't like owls:
A handful of acorns after the cowls!"

But Clarel, bantered by the song,
Sad questioned, if in frames of thought
And feeling, there be right and wrong;
Whether the lesson Joel taught
Confute what from the marble's caught
In sylvan sculpture—Bacchant, Faun,
Or shapes more lax by Titian drawn.
Such counter natures in mankind—
Mole, bird, not more unlike we find:
Instincts adverse, nor less how true
Each to itself. What clew, what clew?

Canto XXI - In Confidence

Towers twain crown Saba's mountain hight;
And one, with larger outlook bold,
Monks frequent climb or day or night
To peer for Arabs. In the breeze
So the ship's lifted topmen hold

Watch on the blue and silver seas,
To guard against the slim Malay,
That perilous imp whose slender proa
Great hulls have rued—as in ill hour
The whale the sword-fish' lank assay.

Upon that pile, to catch the dawn,
Alert next day see Derwent stand
With Clarel. All the mountain-land
Disclosed through Kedron far withdrawn,
Cloven and shattered, hushed and banned,
Seemed poised as in a chaos true,
Or throe-lock of transitional earth
When old forms are annulled, and new
Rebel, and pangs suspend the birth.
That aspect influenced Clarel. Fair
Derwent's regard played other where—
Expectant. Twilight gray took on
Suffusion faint of cherry tone.
The student marked it; but the priest
Marked whence it came: "Turn, turn—the East!
Oh, look! how like an ember red
The seed of fire, by early hand
Raked forth from out the ashy bed,
Shows yon tinged flake of dawn. See, fanned
As 'twere, by this spice-air that blows,
The live coal kindles—the fire grows!"
And mute, he watched till all the East
Was flame: "Ah, who would not here come,
And from dull drowsiness released,
Behold morn's rosy martyrdom!"
It was an unaffected joy,
And showed him free from all annoy
Within—such, say, as mutiny
Of non-content in random touch
That he perchance had overmuch
Favored the first night's revelry.
For Clarel—though at call indeed
He might not else than turn and feed
On florid dawn—not less, anon,
When wonted light of day was won,
Sober and common light, with that
Returned to him his unelate
And unalleviated tone;
And thoughts, strange thoughts, derived overnight,
Touching the Swede's dark undelight,
Recurred; with sequence how profuse
Concerning all the company—

The Arnaut, and the man of glee—
The Lesbian, and calm grave Druze,
And Belex; yes, and in degree
Even Rolfe; Vine too. Less he who trim
Beside him stood, eludes his doubt—
Derwent himself, whose easy skim
Never had satisfied throughout.
He now, if not deemed less devout
Through wassail and late hint of him,
Was keenlier scanned. Yet part might be
Effect of long society,
Which still detracts. But in review
Of one who could such doubt renew,
Clarel inveighs: Parhelion orb
Of faith autumnal, may the dew
Of earth's sad tears thy rays absorb?
Truth bitter: Derwent bred distrust
Heavier than came from Mortmain's thrust
Into the cloud—profounder far
Than Achor's glen with ominous scar.
All aliens now being quite aloof,
Fain would he put that soul to proof.
Yet, fearful lest he might displease,
His topics broached he by degrees.
Needless. For Derwent never shrunk:
"Lad, lad, this diffidence forget;
Believe, you talk here to no monk:
Who's old Duns Scotus? We're well met.

Glad that at last your mind you set
In frank communion here with me.
Better had this been earlier, though;
There lacked not times of privacy
Had such been sought. But yes, I know;
You're young, you're off the poise; and so
A link have felt with hearts the same
Though more advanced. I scarce can blame.
And yet perhaps one here might plead
These rather stimulate than feed.
Nor less let each tongue say its say;
Therefrom we truth elicit. Nay,
And with the worst, 'tis understood
We broader clergy think it good
No more to use censorious tone:
License to all.—We are alone;
Speak out, that's right."
                    The student first
Cited the din of clashed belief

So loud in Palestine, and chief
By Calvary, where are rehearsed
Within the Sepulcher's one fane
All rituals which, ere Luther's reign,
Shared the assent of Christendom.
Besides: how was it even at home?
Behind the mellow chancel's rail
Lurked strife intestine. What avail
The parlor-chapels liberal?
The hearers their own minds elect;
The very pews are each a sect;
No one opinion's steadfast sway:
A wide, an elemental fray.
As with ships moored in road unsafe,
When gales augment and billows chafe,
Hull drives 'gainst hull, endangering all
In crossing cables; while from thrall
Of anchor, others, dragged amain,
Drift seaward: so the churches strain,
Much so the fleets sectarian meet
Doubt's equinox. Yes, all was dim;
He saw no one secure retreat;
Of late so much had shaken him.
Derwent in grave concern inclined.
"Part true, alas!" Nor less he claimed
Reserves of solace, and of kind
Beyond that in the desert named,
When the debate was scarce with men
Who owned with him a common ground—
True center where they might convene.
And yet this solace when unbound
At best proved vague (so Clarel deemed).
He thought, too, that the priest here seemed
Embarrassed on the sudden, nay,
He faltered. What could so betray?
In single contact, heart to heart,
With young, fresh, fervid earnestness,
Was he surprised into distress—
An honest quandary, a smart
More trying e'en than Mortmain's dart,
Grieving and graveling, could deal?
But Derwent rallied, and with zeal:
"Shall everything then plain be made?
Not that there's any ambuscade:
In youth's first heat to think to know!
For time 'tis well to bear a cross:
Yet on some waters here below
Pilots there be, if one's at loss."

The pupil colored; then restrained
An apt retort too personal,
Content with this: "Pilots retained?
But in debates which I recall
Such proved but naught. This side that side,
They crossing hail through fogs that dwell
Upon a limitless deep tide,
While their own cutters toll the bell
Of groping."
Derwent bit the lip;
Altered again, had fain let slip
"Throw all this burden upon HIM;"

But hesitated. Changing trim,
Considerate then he turned a look
Which seemed to weigh as in a book
Just how far youth might well be let
Into maturity's cabinet.
He, as in trial, took this tone:
"Not but there's here and there a heart
Which shares at whiles strange throbs alone.
Such at the freakish sting will start:
No umpirage! they cry—we dote
To dream heaven drops a casting vote,
In these perplexities takes part!"

Clarel, uncertain, stood at gaze,
But Derwent, riving that amaze,
Advanced impulsively: "Your hand!
No longer will I be restrained.
Yours is a sect—but never mind:
By function we are intertwined,
Our common function. Weigh it thus:
Clerics we are clerics, my son;
Nay, shrink not so incredulous;
Paternally my sympathies run—
Toward you I yearn. Well, now: what joy,
What saving calm, what but annoy
In all this hunt without one clew?
What lack ye, pray? what would ye do?
Have Faith, which, even from the myth,
Draws something to be useful with:
In any form some truths will hold;
Employ the present-sanctioned mold.
Nay, hear me out; clean breast I make,
Quite unreserved—and for whose sake?
Suppose an instituted creed
(Or truth or fable) should indeed

To ashes fall; the spirit exhales,
But reinfunds in active forms:
Verse, popular verse, it charms or warms—
Bellies Philosophy's flattened sails—
Tinctures the very book, perchance,
Which claims arrest of its advance.
Why, the true import, deeper use
Shows first when Reason quite slips noose,
And Faith's long dead. Attest that gold
Which Bacon counted down and told
In one ripe tract, by time unshamed,
Wherein from riddle he reclaimed
The myths of Greece. But go back—well,
Reach to the years of first decay
Or totter: prithee, lad, but tell
How with the flamens of that day?
When brake the sun from morning's tents
And walked the hills, and gilded thence
The fane in porch; the priest in view
Bowed—hailed Apollo, as before,
Ere change set in; what else to do?
Or whither turn, or what adore?
What but to temporize for him,
Stranded upon an interim
Between the ebb and flood? He knew.—
You see? Transfer—apply it, you."
"Ill know I what you there advise.—
Ah, heaven!" and for a moment stood;
Then turned: "A rite they solemnize
An awful rite, and yet how sweet
To humble hearts which sorrows beat.
Tell, is that mystic flesh and blood—
I shrink to utter it!—Of old
For medicine they mummy sold—
Conjurer's balsam.—God, my God,
Sorely Thou triest me the clod!"

Upon the impassioned novice here
Discreet the kind proficient throws
The glance of one who still would peer
Where best to take the hedge or close.
Ere long: "You'd do the world some good?
Well, then: no good man will gainsay
That good is good, done any way,
In any name, by any brotherhood.
How think you there?"
From Clarel naught.
Derwent went on: "For lamp you yearn—

A lantern to benighted thought.
Obtain it—whither will you turn?
Still lost you'd be in blanks of snow.
My fellow-creature, do you know
That what most satisfies the head
Least solaces the heart? Less light
Than warmth needs earthly wight.
Christ built a hearth:the flame is dead
We'll say, extinct; but lingers yet,
Enlodged in stone, the hoarded heat.
Why not nurse that? Would rive the door
And let the sleet in? But, once o'er,
This tarrying glow, never to man,
Methinks, shall come the like again.
What if some camp on crags austere
The Stoic held ere Gospel cheer?
There may the common herd abide,
Having dreamed of heaven? Nay, and can you?
You shun that; what shall needier do?
Think, think!"
The student, sorely tried,
The appeal and implication felt,
But comfort none.
And Derwent dealt
Heaped measure still: "All your ado
In youth was mine; your swarm I knew
Of buzzing doubts. But is it good
Such gnats to fight? or well to brood
In selfish introverted search,
Leaving the poor world in the lurch?
Not so did Christ. Nor less he knew
And shared a troubled era too;
And shared besides that problem gray
Which is forever and alway:
His person our own shadow threw.
Then heed him, heed his eldership:
In all respects did Christ indeed
Credit the Jews' crab-apple creed
Whereto he yet conformed? or so
But use it, graft it with his slip
From Paradise? No, no—no, no!
Spare fervid speech! But, for the rest,
Be not extreme. Midway is best.
Herein 'tis never as by Nile
From waste to garden but a stile.
Betwixt rejection and belief,
Shadings there are—degrees, in brief.
But ween you, gentle friend, your way

Of giving to yourself the goad
Is obsolete, no more the mode?
Our comrades—frankly let me say—
That Rolfe, good fellow though he be,
And Vine, methinks, would you but see,
Are much like prints from plates but old.
Interpretations so unfold—
New finding, happy gloss or key,
A decade's now a century.
Byron's storm-cloud away has rolled—
Joined Werter's; Shelley's drowned; and—why,
Perverse were now e'en Hamlet's sigh:
Perverse?—indecorous indeed!"
"E'en so? e'en sadly is it so?"
"Not sad, but veritable, know.
But what—how's this!" For here, with speed
Of passion, Clarel turned: "Forbear!
Ah, wherefore not at once name Job,
In whom these Hamlets all conglobe.
Own, own with me, and spare to feign,
Doubt bleeds, nor Faith is free from pain!"
Derwent averted here his face
With his own heart he seemed to strive;
Then said: "Alas, too deep you dive.
But hear me yet for little space:
This shaft you sink shall strike no bloom:
The surface, ah, heaven keeps that green;
Green, sunny: nature's active scene,
For man appointed, man's true home."

He ended. Saba's desert lay—
Glare rived by gloom. That comment's sway
He felt: "Our privacy is gone;
Here trips young Anselm to espy
Arab or pilgrim drawing nigh.
Dost hear him? come then, we'll go down.
Precede. "
At every step and steep,
While higher came the youthful monk,
Lower and lower in Clarel sunk
The freighted heart. It touched this deep:
Ah, Nehemiah, alone art true?
Secure in reason's wane or loss?
Thy folly that folly of the cross
Contemned by reason, yet how dear to you?

Canto XXII - The Medallion

In Saba, as by one consent,
Frequent the pilgrims single went;
So, parting with his young compeer,
And breaking fast without delay,
For more restorative and cheer,
Good Derwent lightly strolled away
Within this monkish capital.
Chapels and oratories all,
And shrines in coves of gilded gloom;
The kitchen, too, and pantler's room—
Naught came amiss.
Anear the church
He drew unto a kind of porch
Such as next some old minsters be,
An inner porch (named Galilee
In parlance of the times gone by),
A place for discipline and grief.
And here his tarry had been brief
But for a shield of marble nigh,
Set in the living rock: a stone
In low relief, where well was shown,
Before an altar under sky,
A man in armor, visor down,
Enlocked complete in panoply,
Uplifting reverent a crown
In invocation.
This armed man
In corselet showed the dinted plate,
And dread streaks down the thigh-piece ran;
But the bright helm inviolate
Seemed raised above the battle-zone—
Cherubic with a rare device;
Perch for the Bird-of-Paradise.
A victor seemed he, without pride
Of victory, or joy in fame:
'Twas reverence, and naught beside,
Unless it might that shadow claim
Which comes of trial. Yes, the art
So cunning was, that it in part
By fair expressiveness of grace
Atoned even for the visored face.

Long time becharmed here Derwent stood,
Charmed by the marble's quiet mood
Of beauty, more than by its tone
Of earnestness, though these were one

In that good piece. Yes, long he fed
Ere yet the eye was lower led
To trace the inscription underrun:
O fair and friendly manifested Spirit!
Before thine altar dear
Let me recount the marvel of the story
Fulfilled in tribute here.

In battle waged where all was fraudful silence,
Foul battle against odds,
Disarmed, I, fall'n and trampled, prayed: Death, so
Come, Death: thy hand is God's!

A pale hand noiseless from the turf responded,
Riving the turf and stone:
It raised, re-armed me, sword and golden armor,
And waved me warring on.

O fairest, friendliest, and ever holy—
O Love, dissuading fate—
To thee, to thee the rescuer, thee sainted,
The crown I dedicate:

To thee I dedicate the crown, a guerdon
The winner may not wear;
His wound re-opens, and he goes to haven:
Spirit! befriend him there.

"A hero, and shall he repine?
'Tis not Achilles;" and straightway
He felt the charm in sort decline;
And, turning, saw a votary gray:
"Good brother, tell: make this thing clear:
Who set this up?" "'Twas long ago,
Yes, long before I harbored here,
Long centuries, they say." "Why, no!
So bright it looks, 'tis recent, sure.
Who set it up?" "A count turned monk."
"What count?" "His name he did abjure
For Lazarus, and ever shrunk
From aught of his life's history:
Yon slab tells all or nothing, see.
But this I've heard; that when the stone
Hither was brought from Cyprus fair
(Some happy sculptors flourished there
When Venice ruled), he said to one:
'They've made the knight too rich appear—
Too rich in helm.' He set it here

In Saba as securest place,
For a memorial of grace
To outlast him, and many a year."

'Tis travel teaches much that's strange,
Mused Derwent in his further range;
Then fell into uneasy frame:
The visored man, relinquished name,
And touch of unglad mystery.

He rallied: I will go and see
The archimandrite in his court:
And thither straight he made resort
And met with much benignity.

The abbot's days were near the span,
A holy and right reverend man,
By name Christodulus, which means
Servant of Christ. Behind the screens
He kept, but issued the decree:
Unseen he ruled, and sightlessly:
Yes, blind he was, stone-blind and old;
But, in his silken vestment rolled,
At mid-day on his Persian rug,
Showed cosy as the puss Maltese
Demure, in rosy fire-light snug,
Upon the velvet hem at ease
Of seated lady's luxuries
Of robe. For all his days, and nights,
Which Eld finds wakeful, and the slights
Of churlish Time, life still could please.
And chief what made the charm to be,
Was his retention of that toy,
Dear to the old—authority.
And blent herewith was soothing balm,
Senior complacency of calm—

A settledness without alloy,
In tried belief how orthodox
And venerable; which the shocks
Of schism had stood, ere yet the state
Of Peter claimed earth's pastorate.
So far back his Greek Church did plant,
Rome's Pope he deemed but Protestant—

A Rationalist, a bigger Paine—
Heretic, worse than Arian;
He lumped him with that compound mass
Of sectaries of the West, alas!

Breathed Derwent: "This is a lone life;
Removed thou art from din and strife,

But from all news as well."
"Even so,
My son. But what's news here below?
For hearts that do Christ's promise claim,
No hap's important since He came.
Besides: in Saba here remain
Ten years; then back, the world regain—
Five minutes' talk with any one
Would put thee even with him, son.
Pretentious are events, but vain."
"But new books, authors of the time?"
"Books have we ever new—sublime:
The Scriptures—drama, precept fine,
Verse and philosophy divine,
All best. Believe again, O son,
God's revelation, Holy Writ,
Quite supersedes and makes unfit
All text save comment thereupon.
The Fathers have we, these discuss:
Sweet Chrysostom, Basilius,
Great Athanase, and—but all's known
To you, no question."
In the mien
Of Derwent, as this dropped in ear,
A junior's deference was seen.
Nothing he controverted. Here
He won the old man's heart, he knew,
And readier brought to pass the thing
That he designed: which was, to view
The treasures of this hermit-king.
At hint urbane, the abbot called
An acolyth, a blue-robed boy,
So used to service, he forestalled
His lighter wishes, and took joy
In serving. Keys were given. He took
From out a coffer's deeper nook
Small shrines and reliquaries old:
Beryl and Indian seed-pearl set
In little folding-doors of gold
And ivory, of tryptych form,

With starred Byzantine pictures warm,
And opening into cabinet
Where lay secured in precious zone
The honeycombed gray-greenish bone
Of storied saint. But prized supreme
Were some he dwelt upon, detained,
Felt of them lovingly in hand;
Making of such a text or theme
For grave particulars; far back
Tracing them in monastic dream:
While fondling them (in way, alack,
Of Jew his coins) with just esteem
For rich encasings. Here anew
Derwent's attention was not slack;
Yet underneath a reverence due,
Slyly he kept his pleasant state:
The dowager—her family plate.
The abbot, with a blind man's way
Of meek divining, guessed the play
Of inkept comment: "Son," said he,
"These dry bones cannot live: what then?
In times ere Christianity
By worldlings was professed, true men
And brave, which sealed their faith in blood
Or flame, the Christian brotherhood
Revered—attended them in death;
Caught the last parting of the breath:
Happy were they could they but own
Some true memento, but a bone
Purchased from executioner,
Or begged: hence relics. Trust me, son,
'Twas love began, and pious care
Prolongs this homage." Derwent bowed;
And, bland: "Have miracles been wrought
From these?" "No, none by me avowed
From knowledge personal. But then
Such things may be, for they have been."
"Have been?" "'Tis in the Scripture taught
That contact with Elisha's bones
Restored the dead to life." "Most true,"
Eyeing the bits of skeletons
As in enlightened reverence new,
Forgetting that his host was blind,
Nor might the flattery receive.

Erelong, observing the old man
Waxed weary, and to doze began,
Strange settling sidelong, half reclined,

His blessing craved he, and took leave.

Canto XXIV - Vault and Grotto

But Clarel, bides he still by tower?
His was no sprightly frame; nor mate
He sought: it was his inner hour.
Yes, keeping to himself his state,
Nor thinking to break fast till late,
He moved along the gulf's built flank
Within the inclosures rank o'er rank.
Accost was none, for none he saw,
Until the Druze he chanced to meet,
Smoking, nor did the Emir draw
The amber from the mouth, to greet,
Not caring so to break the spell
Of that Elysian interval;
But lay, his pipe at lengthy lean,
Reclined along the crag serene,
As under Spain's San Pedro dome
The long-sword Cid upon his tomb;
And with an unobtrusive eye
Yet apprehending, and mild mien,
Regarded him as he went by
Tossed in his trouble. 'Twas a glance
Clarel did many a time recall,
Though its unmeant significance
That was the last thing learned of all.

But passing on by ways that wind,
A place he gained secluded there
In ledge. A cenobite inclined
Busy at scuttle-hole in floor
Of rock, like smith who may repair
A bolt of Mammon's vault. The door
Or stony slab lay pushed aside.
Deeming that here the monks might store,
In times of menace which they bide,
Their altar plate, Clarel drew near,
But faltered at the friar's sad tone
Ascetical. He looked like one
Whose life is but a patience mere,
Or worse, a fretting doubt of cheer
Beyond; he toiled as in employ
Imposed, a bondman far from joy.
No answer made he to salute,

Yet deaf might be. And now, while mute
The student lingered, lo, down slipped
Through cleft of crags, the sun did win
Aloft in Kedron's citadel,
A fiery shaft into that crypt
(Like well-pole slant in farm-house well)
And lighted it: and he looked in.
On stony benches, head by head,
In court where no recorders be,
Preserved by nature's chemistry
Sat the dim conclave of the dead,
Encircled where the shadow rules,
By sloping theatres of skulls.
He rose retreated by the line
Of cliff, but paused at tones which sent:
"So pale? the end's nor imminent
Nor far. Stand, thou; the countersign!"—
It came from over Kedron's rent.
Thitherward then his glance he bent,
And saw, by mouth of grot or mine,
Rustic with wicket's rude design,
A sheeted apparition wait,
Like Lazarus at the charnel gate
In Bethany.
                    "The countersign!"
"Reply, say something; yea, say Death, "
Prompted the monk, erewhile so mute.
Clarel obeyed; and, in a breath,
"Advance!" the shroud cried, turning foot,
And so retired there into gloom
Within, and all again was dumb.
"And who that man—or ghost?" he yearned
Unto the toiler; who returned:
"Cyril. 'Tis long since that he craved
Over against to dwell encaved.
In youth he was a soldier. Go."
But Clarel might not end it so:
"I pray thee, friend, what grief or zeal
Could so unhinge him? that reveal."
"Go—ask your world:" and grim toiled on,
Fitting his clamp as if alone,
Dismissing him austerely thus.
And Clarel, sooth, felt timorous.
Conscious of seeds within his frame
Transmitted from the early gone,
Scarce in his heart might he disclaim
That challenge from the shrouded one.
He walked in vision—saw in fright

Where through the limitless of night
The spirits innumerable lie,
Strewn like snared miners in vain flight
From the dull black-damp. Die—to die!
To be, then not to be! to end,
And yet time never, never suspend
His going.—This is cowardice
To brood on this!—Ah, Ruth, thine eyes
Abash these base mortalities!
But slid the change, anew it slid
As by the Dead Sea marge forbid:
The vision took another guise:
From 'neath the closing, lingering lid
Ruth's glance of love is glazing met,
Reproaching him: Dost tarry, tarry yet?

Canto XXV - Derwent and the Lesbian

If where, in blocks unbeautified,
But lath and plaster may divide
The cot of dole from bed of bride;
Here, then, a page's slender shell
Is thick enough to set between
The graver moral, lighter mien—
The student and the cap-and-bell.
'Tis nature.
Pastime to achieve,
After he reverent did leave
The dozer in the gallery,
Derwent, good man of pleasantry,
He sauntered by the stables old,
And there the ass spied through a door,
Lodged in a darksome stall or hold,
The head communing with the floor.
Taking some barley, near at hand,
He entered, but was brought to stand,
Hearing a voice: "Don't bother her;

She cares not, she, for provender;
Respect her nunnery, her cell:
She's pondering, see, the asses' hell."
He turned; it was the Lesbian wag,
Who offered straight to be his guide
Even anywhere, be it vault or crag.
"Well, thanks; but first to feed your nun,
She fasts overmuch.—There, it is done.

Come show me, do, that famous tide
Evoked up from the waste, they tell,
The canonized abbot's miracle,
St. Saba's fount: where foams it, pray?"
"Near where the damned ones den." "What say?"

"Down, plummets down. But come along;"
And leading, whiled the way with song:
"Saintly lily, credit me,
Sweet is the thigh of the honey-bee!
Ruddy ever and oleose,
Ho for the balm of the red, red rose!"

Stair after stair, and stair again,
And ladder after ladder free,
Lower and steeper, till the strain
Of cord irked Derwent: "Verily,
E'en as but now you lightly said,
'Tis to Avernus we are bending;
And how much further this descending?"
At last they dropped down on the bed
Of Kedron, sought a cavern dead
And there the fount.
"'Tis cool to sip,
I'm told; my cup, here 'tis; wilt dip?"
And proffered it: "With me, with me,
Alas, this natural dilution
Of water never did agree;
Mine is a touchy constitution;
'Tis a respectable fluid though.
Ah, you don't care. Well, come out, do.
The thing to mark here's not the well,
But Saba in her crescent swell,
Terrace on terrace piled. And see,
Up there by yon small balcony
Our famous palm stands sentinel.
Are you a good believer?" "Why?"
"Because that blessed tree (not I,
But all our monks avouch it so)
Was set a thousand years ago
By dibble in St. Saba's hand."
"Indeed? Heaven crown him for it. Palm!
Thou benediction in the land,
A new millennium may'st thou stand:
So fair, no fate would do thee harm."
Much he admired the impressive view;
Then facing round and gazing up
Where soared the crags: "Yon grottoes few

Which make the most ambitious group
Of all the laura row on row,
Can one attain?" "Forward!" And so
Up by a cloven rift they plied—
Saffron and black—branded beside,
Like to some felon's wall of cell
Smoked with his name. Up they impel
Till Derwent, overwearied, cried:
"Dear Virgil mine, you are so strong,
But I, thy Dante, am nigh dead."
"Who daunts ye, friend? don't catch the thread."
"The ascending path was ever long."
"Ah yes; well, cheer it with a song:
"My love but she has little feet
And slippers of the rose,
From under—Oh, the lavender sweet—
Just peeping out, demurely neat;
But she, she never knows—
No, no, she never knows!

"A dimpled hand is hers, and e'en
As dainty as her toes;
In mine confiding it she'll lean
Till heaven knows what my tinglings mean;
But she, she never knows—
Oh no, she never knows!

"No, never!—Hist!"
"Nay, revelers, stay.
Lachryma Christi makes ye glad!
Where joys he now shall next go mad?
His snare the spider weaves in sun:
But ye, your lease has yet to run;
Go, go: from ye no countersign."

Such incoherence! where lurks he,
The ghoul, the riddler? in what mine?
It came from an impending crag
Or cleft therein, or cavity.
The man of bins a bit did drag;
But quick to Derwent, "Never lag:
A crazy friar; but prithee, haste:
I know him,—Cyril; there, we've passed."
"Well, that is queer—the queerest thing,"
Said Derwent, breathing nervously.
"He's ever ready with his sting,
Though dozing in his grotto dull."
"Demented—pity! let him be."

"Ay, if he like that kind of hull,
Let the poor wasp den in the skull."
"What's that?" here Derwent; "that shrill cry?"
And glanced aloft; "for mercy, look!"
A great bird crossed high up in sky
Over the gulf; and, under him,
Its downward flight a black thing took,
And, eddying by the path's sheer rim,
Still spun below: "'Tis Mortmain's cap,
The skull-cap!" "Skull is't? say ye skull
From heaven flung into Kedron's lap?
The gods were ever bountiful!
No—there: I see. Small as a wren—
That death's head of all mortal men—
Look where he's perched on topmost crag,
Bareheaded brooding. Oh, the hag,
That from the very brow could pluck
The cap of a philosopher
So near the sky, then, with a mock,
Disdain and drop it." "Queer, 'tis queer
Indeed!" "One did the same to me,
Yes, much the same—pecked at my hat,
I mountain-riding, dozingly,
Upon a dromedary drear.
The devil's in these eagles-gier.
She ones they are, be sure of that,
That be so saucy.—Ahoy there, thou!"
Shooting the voice in sudden freak
Athwart the chasm, where wended slow
The timoneer, that pilgrim Greek,
The graybeard in the mariner trim,
The same that told the story o'er
Of crazy compass and the Moor.
But he, indeed, not hearing him,
Pursued his way.
"That salted one,
That pickled old sea-Solomon,
Tempests have deafened him, I think.
He has a tale can make ye wink;
And pat it comes in too. But dwell!
Here. sit we down here while I tell."

Canto XXVI - Vine and the Palm

Along those ledges, up and down—
Through terce, sext, nones, in ritual flight

To vespers and mild evening brown;
On errand best to angels known,
A shadow creepeth, brushed by light.
Behold it stealing now over one
Reclined aloof upon a stone
High up. 'Tis Vine.
            And is it I
(He muses), I that leave the others,
Or do they leave me? One could sigh
For Achmed with his hundred brothers:
How share the gushing amity
With all? Divine philanthropy!
For my part, I but love the past—
The further back the better; yes,
In the past is the true blessedness;
The future's ever overcast—
The present aye plebeian. So,
Mar Saba, thou fine long-ago
Lithographed here, thee do I love;
And yet to-morrow I'll remove
With right good will; a fickle lover
Is only constant as a rover.
Here I lie, poor solitaire;
But see the brave one over there-
The Palm! Come now, to pass the time
I'll try an invocation free
Invoke it in a style sublime,
Yet sad as sad sincerity:—
"Witness to a watered land,
Voucher of a vernal year—
St. Saba's Palm, why there dost stand?
Would'st thou win the desert here
To dreams of Eden? Thy device
Intimates a Paradise!
Nay, thy plume would give us proof
That thou thyself art prince thereof,
Fair lord of that domain.
"But, lonely dwelling in thy reign,
Kinship claimest with the tree
Worshipped on Delos in the sea—
Apollo's Palm? It ended;
Nor dear divinities befriended.—
"Thou that pledgest heaven to me,
Stem of beauty, shaft of light,
Behold, thou hang'st suspended
Over Kedron and the night!
Shall come the fall? shall time disarm
The grace, the glory of the Palm?

"Tropic seraph! thou once gone,
Who then shall take thy office on—
Redeem the waste, and high appear,
Apostle of Talassa's year
And climes where rivers of waters run?
"But braid thy tresses—yet thou'rt fair:
Every age for itself must care:
Braid thy green tresses; let the grim
Awaiter find thee never dim!
Serenely still thy glance be sent
Plumb down from horror's battlement:
Though the deep Fates be concerting
A reversion, a subyerting,
Still bear thee like the Seraphim."

He loitered, lounging on the stair:
Howbeit, the sunlight still is fair.
Next meetly here behooves narrate
How fared they, seated left but latc
Viewless to Vine above their dell,
Viewless and quite inaudible:
Derwent, and his good gossip cosy,
The man of Lesbos, light and rosy,
His anecdote about to tell.

Canto XXVII - Man and Bird

"Yes, pat it comes in here for me:
He says, that one fine day at sea—
'Twas when he younger was and spry—
Being at mast-head all alone,
While he his business there did ply,
Strapping a block where halyards run,
He felt a fanning overhead—
Looked up, and so into the eye
Of a big bird, red-billed and black
In plume. It startled him, he said,
It seemed a thing demoniac.
From poise, it went to wheeling round him;
Then, when in daze it well had bound him,
It pounced upon him with a buffet;
He, enraged, essayed to cuff it,
But only had one hand, the other
Still holding on the spar. And so,
While yet they shouted from below,
And yet the wings did whirr and smother,

The bird tore at his old wool cap,
And chanced upon the brain to tap.
Up went both hands; he lost his stay,
And down he fell—he, and the bird
Maintaining still the airy fray—
And, souse, plumped into sea; and heard,
While sinking there, the piercing gird
Of the grim fowl, that bore away
The prize at last."
"And did he drown?"
"Why, there he goes!" and pointed him
Where still the mariner wended on:
"'Twas in smooth water; he could swim.
They luffed and flung the rope, and fired
The harpoon at the shark untired
Astern, and dragged him—not the shark,
But man—they dragged him 'board the barque;
And down he dropped there with a thump,
Being water-logged with spongy lump
Of quilted patches on the shirt
Of wool, and trowsers. All inert
He lay. He says, and true's the word,
That bitterer than the brine he drank
Was that shrill gird the while he sank."
"A curious story, who e'er heard
Of such a fray 'twixt man and bird!"—
"Bird? but he deemed it was the devil,
And that he carried off his soul
In the old cap, nor was made whole
'Till some good vicar did unravel
The snarled illusion in the skein,
And he got back his soul again."
"But lost his cap. A curious story—
A bit of Nature's allegory.
And—well, what now? You seem perplexed."
"And so I am.—Your friend there, see,
Up on yon peak, he puzzles me.
Wonder where I shall find him next?
Last time 'twas where the corn-cribs by
Bone-cribs, I mean; in church, you know;

The blessed martyrs' holy bones,
Hard by the porch as in you go—
Sabaites' bones, the thousand ones
Of slaughtered monks—so faith avers.
Dumb, peering in there through the bars
He stood. Then, in the spiders' room,
I saw him there, yes, quite at home

In long-abandoned library old,
Conning a venerable tome,
While dust of ages round him rolled;
Nor heeded he the big fly's buzz,
But mid heaped parchment leaves that mold
Sat like the bankrupt man of Uz
Among the ashes, and read and read.
Much learning, has it made him mad?
Kedron well suits him, 'twould appear:
Why don't he stay, yes, anchor here,
Turn anchorite?"
And do ye pun,
And he, he such an austere one?
(Thought Derwent then.) Well, run your rig—
Hard to be comic and revere;
And once 'twas tittered in mine ear
St. Paul himself was but a prig.
Who's safe from the derision.?—Here
Aloud: "Why, yes; our friend is queer,
And yet, as some esteem him, not
Without some wisdom to his lot."
"Wisdom? our Cyril is deemed wise.
In the East here, one who's lost his wits
For saint or sage they canonize:
That's pretty good for perquisites.
I'll tell you: Cyril (some do own)
Has gained such prescience as to man
(Through seldom seeing any one),
To him's revealed the mortal span
Of any wight he peers upon.
And that's his hobby—as we proved
But late.

"Then not in vain we've roved,
Winning the oracle whose caprice
Avers we've yet to run our lease."
"Length to that lease! But let's return,
Give over climbing, and adjourn."
"Just as you will."
"But first to show
A curious caverned place hard by.
Another crazed monk—start not so—
He's gone, clean vanished from the eye!
Another crazed one, deemed inspired,
Long dwelt in it. He never tired—
Ah, here it is, the vestibule."

They reach an inner grotto cool,

Lighted by fissure up in dome;
Fixed was each thing, each fixture stone:
Stone bed, bench, cross, and altar—stone.
"How like you it—Habbibi's home?
You see these writings on the wall?
His craze was this: he heard a call
Ever from heaven: O scribe, write, write!
Write this—that write to these indite—
To them! Forever it was—write!
Well, write he did, as here you see.
What is it all?"
                    "Dim, dim to me,"
Said Derwent; "ay, obscurely traced;
And much is rubbed off or defaced.
But here now, this is pretty clear:
'I, Self I am the enemy
Of all. From me deliver me,
O Lord. '—Poor man!—But here, dim here:
'There is a hell over which mere hell
Serves—for—a—heaven.'—Oh, terrible!
Profound pit that must be!—What's here
Halffaded: '. . . teen . . six,
The hundred summers run,
Except it be in cicatrix
The aloe—flowers—none.'—
Ah, Nostradamus; prophecy
Is so explicit.—But this, see.
Much blurred again: '. . . testimony,
. . . . . grown fat and gray,
The lion down, and—full of honey,
The bears shall rummage—him—in—May.'—
Yes, bears like honey.—Yon gap there
Well lights the grotto; and this air
Is dry and sweet; nice citadel
For study."
              "Or dessert-room. So,
Hast seen enough? then let us go.
Write, write—indite!—what peer you at?"
Emerging, Derwent, turning round,
Small text spied which the door-way crowned.
"Ha, new to me; and what is that?"
The Islesman asked; "pray read it o'er."
" 'Ye here who enter Habbi's den,
Beware what hence ye take!' " "Amen!
Why didn't he say that before?
But what's to take? all's fixture here."
"Occult, occult," said Derwent, "queer.
Returning now, they made descent,

The pilot trilling as they went:
"King Cole sang as he clinked the can,
Sol goes round, and the mill-horse too:
A thousand pound for a fire-proof man!
The devil vows he's the sole true-blue;
And the prick-louse sings,
See the humbug of kings—
'Tis I take their measure, ninth part of a man!"

Lightly he sheds it off (mused then
The priest), a man for Daniel's den.
In by-place now they join the twain,
Belex, and Og in red Fez bald;
And Derwent, in his easy vein
Ear gives to chat, with wine and gladness,
Pleased to elude the Siddim madness,
And, yes, even that in grotto scrawled;
Nor grieving that each pilgrim friend
For time now leave him to unbend.
Yet, intervening even there,
A touch he knew of gliding care:
We loiterers whom life can please
(Thought he) could we but find our mates
Ever! but no; before the gates
Of joy, lie some who carp and tease:
Collisions of men's destinies!—
But quick, to nullify that tone
He turned to mark the jovial one
Telling the twain, the martial pair,
Of Cairo and his tarry there;
And how, his humorous soul to please,
He visited the dervishes,
The dancing ones: "But what think ye?
The captain-dervish vowed to me
That those same cheeses, whirl-round-rings
He made, were David's—yes, the king's
Who danced before the Ark. But, look:
This was the step King David took;"
And cut fantastic pigeon-wings.

Canto XXVIII - Mortmain and the Palm

"See him!—How all your threat he braves,
Saba! your ominous architraves
Impending, stir him not a jot.
Scarce he would change with me in lot:

Wiser am I?—Curse on this store
Of knowledge! Nay, 'twas cursed of yore.
Knowledge is power: tell that to knaves;
'Tis knavish knowledge: the true lore
Is impotent for earth: 'Thyself
Thou can'st not save; come down from cross!'
They cast it in His teeth; trim Pelf
Stood by, and jeered, Is gold then dross?—
Cling to His tree, and there find hope:
Me it but makes a misanthrope.
Makes? nay, but 't would, did not the hate
Dissolve in pity of the fate.—
This legend, dream, and fact of life!
The drooping hands, the dancing feet
Which in the endless series meet;
And rumors of No God so rife!"

The Swede, the brotherless—who else?
'Twas he, upon the brink opposed,
To whom the Lesbian was disclosed
In antic: hence those syllables.

Ere long (at distance from that scene)
A voice dropped on him from a screen
Above: "Ho, halt!" It chanced to be
The challenged here no start incurred,
Forewarned of near vicinity
Of Cyril and his freak. He heard,
Looked up, and answered, "Well?" "The word!"
"Hope," in derision. "Stand, delay:
That was pass-word for yesterday."

"Despair." "Advance."
He, going, scanned
The testimony of the hand
Gnawed in the dream: "Yea, but 'tis here.
Despair? nay, death; and what's death's cheer?
Death means—the sea-beat gains the shore;
He's home; his watch is called no more.
So looks it. Not I tax thee, Death,
With that, which might make Strength a trembler,—
While yet for me it scants no breath—
That, quiet under sleepiest mound,
Thou art a dangerous dissembler;
That he whose evil is profound
In multiform of life's disguises,
Whom none dare check, and naught chastises,
And in his license thinks no bound—

For him thou hoardest strange surprises!—
But what—the Tree? O holy Palm,
If 'tis a world where hearts wax warm
Oftener through hate than love, and chief
The bland thing be the adder's charm,
And the true thing virtue's ancient grief—
Thee yet it nourishes—even thee!
"Envoy, whose looks the pang assuage,
Disclose thy heavenly embassage!
That lily-rod which Gabriel bore
To Mary, kneeling her before,
Announcing a God, the mother she;
That budded stalk from Paradise—
Like that thou shin'st in thy device:
And sway'st thou over here toward me—
Toward me can such a symbol sway!"

In rounded turn of craggy way,
Across the interposed abyss,
He had encountered it. Submiss,
He dropped upon the under stone,
And soon in such a dream was thrown
He felt as floated up in cheer
Of saint borne heavenward from the bier.
Indeed, each wakeful night, and fast
(That feeds and keeps what clay would clutch)
With thrills which he did still outlast,
His fibres made so fine in end
That though in trials fate can lend
Firm to withstand, strong to contend;
Sensitive he to a spirit's touch.

A wind awakened him—a breath.
He lay like light upon the heath,
Alive though still. And all came back,
The years outlived, with all their black;
While bright he saw the angel-tree
Across the gulf alluring sway:
Come over! be—forever be
As in the trance.—"Wilt not delay?
Yet hear me in appeal to thee:
When the last light shall fade from me,
If, groping round, no hand I meet;
Thee I'll recall—invoke thee, Palm:
Comfort me then, thou Paraclete!
The lull late mine beneath thy lee,
Then, then renew, and seal the calm."

Upon the ledge of hanging stair,
And under Vine, invisible there,
With eyes still feeding on the Tree,
Relapsed he lingered as in Lethe's snare.

Canto XXIX - Rolfe and the Palm

Pursued, the mounted robber flies
Unawed through Kedron's plunged demesne:
The clink, and clinking echo dies:
He vanishes: a long ravine.
And stealthy there, in little chinks
Betwixt or under slab-rocks, slinks
The dwindled amber current lean.

Far down see Rolfe there, hidden low
By ledges slant. Small does he show
(If eagles eye), small and far off
As Mother-Cary's bird in den
Of Cape Horn's hollowing billow-trough,
When from the rail where lashed they bide
The sweep of overcurling tide,—
Down, down, in bonds the seamen gaze
Upon that flutterer in glen
Of waters where it sheltered plays,
While, over it, each briny hight
Is torn with bubbling torrents white
In slant foam tumbling from the snow
Upon the crest; and far as eye
Can range through mist and scud which fly,
Peak behind peak the liquid summits grow.

By chance Rolfe won the rocky stair
At base, and queried if it were
Man's work or nature's, or the twain
Had wrought together in that lane
Of high ascent, so crooked with turns
And flanked by coignes, that one discerns
But links thereof in flights encaved,
Whate'er the point of view. Up, slow
He climbed for little space; then craved
A respite, turned and sat; and, lo,
The Tree in salutation waved
Across the chasm. Remindings swell;
Sweet troubles of emotion mount—
Sylvan reveries, and they well

From memory's Bandusia fount;
Yet scarce the memory alone,
But that and question merged in one:

"Whom weave ye in,
Ye vines, ye palms? whom now, Soolee?
Lives yet your Indian Arcady?
His sunburnt face what Saxon shows—
His limbs all white as lilies be—
Where Eden, isled, impurpled glows
In old Mendanna's sea?
Takes who the venture after me?
"Who now adown the mountain dell
(Till mine, by human foot untrod—
Nor easy, like the steps to hell)
In panic leaps the appalling crag,
Alighting on the cloistral sod
Where strange Hesperian orchards drag,

Walled round by cliff and cascatelle
Arcades of Iris; and though lorn,
A truant ship-boy overworn,
Is hailed for a descended god?
"Who sips the vernal cocoa's cream—
The nereids dimpling in the darkling stream?
For whom the gambol of the tricksy dream—
Even Puck's substantiated scene,
Yea, much as man might hope and more than heaven m;
"And whom do priest and people sue,
In terms which pathos yet shall tone
When memory comes unto her own,
To dwell with them and ever find them true:
'Abide, for peace is here:
Behold, nor heat nor cold we fear,
Nor any dearth: one happy tide
A dance, a garland of the year:
Abide!'
"But who so feels the stars annoy,
Upbraiding him,—how far astray!—
That he abjures the simple joy,
And hurries over the briny world away?
"Renouncer! is it Adam's flight
Without compulsion or the sin?
And shall the vale avenge the slight
By haunting thee in hours thou yet shalt win?"

He tarried. And each swaying fan
Sighed to his mood in threnodies of Pan.

All distant through that afternoon
The student kept, nor might attune
His heart to any steadfast thought
But Ruth—still Ruth, yet strange involved
With every mystery unresolved
In time and fate. In cloud thus caught,
Her image labored like a star
Fitful revealed in midnight heaven
When inland from the sea-coast far
The storm-rack and dark scud are driven.
Words scarce might tell his frame, in sooth:
'Twas Ruth, and oh, much more than Ruth.

That flank of Kedron still he held
Which is built up; and, passing on—
While now sweet peal of chimings swelled
From belfry old, withdrawn in zone—
A way through cloisters deep he won
And winding vaults that slope to hight;
And heard a voice, espied a light
In twinkle through far passage dim,
And aimed for it, a friendly gleam;
And so came out upon the Tree
Mid-poised, and ledge-built balcony
Inrailed, and one who, leaning o'er
Beneath the Palm—from shore to shore
Of Kedron's overwhelming walls
And up and down her gap and grave,
A golden cry sent, such as calls
To creatures which the summons know.
And, launching from crag, tower, and cave
Beatified in flight they go:
St. Saba's doves, in Saba bred.
For wonted bounty they repair,
These convent-pensioners of air;
Fly to their friend; from hand outspread
Or fluttering at his feet are fed.
Some, iridescent round his brow,
Wheel, and with nimbus him endow.
Not fortune's darling here was seen,
But heaven's elect. The robe of blue
So sorted with the doves in hue
Prevailing, and clear skies serene

Without a cloud; so pure he showed—
Of stature tall, in aspect bright—
He looked an almoner of God,
Dispenser of the bread of light.
'Twas not the intellectual air—
Not solely that, though that be fair:
Another order, and more rare—
As high above the Plato mind
As this above the Mammon kind.
In beauty of his port unsealed,
To Clarel part he stood revealed
At first encounter; but the sweet
Small pecking bills and hopping feet
Had previous won; the host urbane,
In courtesy that could not feign,
Mute welcome yielding, and a seat.
It charmed away half Clarel's care,
And charmed the picture that he saw,
To think how like that turtle pair
Which Mary, to fulfill the law,
From Bethlehem to temple brought
For offering; these Saba doves
Seemed natives—not of Venus' court
Voluptuous with wanton wreath—
But colonnades where Enoch roves,
Or walks with God, as Scripture saith.
Nor myrtle here, but sole the Palm
Whose vernal fans take rich release
From crowns of foot-stalks golden warm.
O martyr's scepter, type of peace,
And trouble glorified to calm!
What stillness in the almoner's face:
Nor Fomalhaut more mild may reign
Mellow above the purple main
Of autumn hills. It was a grace
Beyond medallions ye recall.
The student murmured, filial—
"Father," and tremulously gleamed,
"Here, sure, is peace." The father beamed;
The nature of the peace was such
It shunned to venture any touch
Of word. "And yet," went Clarel on
But faltered there. The saint but glanced.
"Father, if Good, 'tis unenhanced:
No life domestic do ye own
Within these walls: woman I miss.
Like cranes, what years from time's abyss
Their flight have taken, one by one,

Since Saba founded this retreat:
In cells here many a stifled moan
Of lonely generations gone;
And more shall pine as more shall fleet."

With dove on wrist, he, robed, stood hushed,
Mused on the bird, and softly brushed.
Scarce reassured by air so mute,
Anxiously Clarel urged his suit.
The celibate let go the dove;
Cooing, it won the shoulder—lit
Even at his ear, as whispering it.
But he one pace made in remove,
And from a little alcove took
A silver-clasped and vellum book;
And turned a leaf, and gave that page
For answer.—
Rhyme, old hermit-rhyme
Composed in Decius' cruel age
By Christian of Thebyean clime:
'Twas David's son, and he of Dan
With him misloved that fled the bride
And Job whose wife but mocked his ban
Then rose, or in redemption ran—
The rib restored to Adam's side
And man made whole, as man began.
And lustral hymns and prayers were here:
Renouncings, yearnings, charges dread
Against our human nature dear:
Worship and wail, which, if misled
Not less might fervor high instill
In hearts which, striving in their fear
Of clay, to bridle, curb or kill;
In the pure desert of the will
Chastised, live the vowed life austere.

The given page the student scanned:
Started—reviewed, nor might withstand.
He turned; the celibate was gone;
Over the gulf he hung alone:
Alone, but for the comment caught
Or dreamed, in face seen far below,
Upturned toward the Palm in thought,
Or else on him—he scarce might know.
Fixed seemed it in assent indeed
Which indexed all? It was the Swede.
Over the Swede, upon the stair—
Long Bethel-stair of ledges brown

Sloping as from the heaven let down—
Apart lay Vine; lowermost there,
Rolfe he discerned; nor less the three,
While of each other unaware,
In one consent of frame might be.
How vaguely, while yet influenced so
By late encounter, and his glance
Rested on Vine, his reveries flow
Recalling that repulsed advance
He knew by Jordan in the wood,
And the enigma unsubdued—
Possessing Ruth, nor less his heart
Aye hungering still, in deeper part
Unsatisfied. Can be a bond
(Thought he) as David sings in strain
That dirges beauteous Jonathan,
Passing the love of woman fond?
And may experience but dull
The longing for it? Can time teach?
Shall all these billows win the lull
And shallow on life's hardened beach?—

He lingered. The last dove had fled,
And nothing breathed—breathed, waved, or fed,
Along the uppermost sublime
Blank ridge. He wandered as in sleep;
A saffron sun's last rays were shed
More still, more solemn waxed the time,
Till Apathy upon the steep
Sat one with Silence and the Dead.

Canto XXXI - The Recoil

"But who was SHE (if Luke attest)
Whom generations hail for blest—
Immaculate though human one;
What diademed and starry Nun—
Bearing in English old the name
And hallowed style of HOLIDAME;
She, She, the Mater of the Rood—
Sprang she from Ruth's young sisterhood?"

On cliffin moonlight roaming out
So Clarel, thrilled by deep dissent,
Revulsion from injected doubt
And many a strange presentiment.

But came ere long profound relapse:
The Rhyme recurred, made voids or gaps
In dear relations; while anew,
From chambers of his mind's review
Emerged the saint, who with the Palm
Shared heaven on earth in gracious calm,
Even as his robe partook the hue.
And needs from that high mentor part?
Is strength too strong to teach the weak?
Though tame the life seem, turn the cheek,
Does the call elect the hero-heart?—
The thunder smites our tropic bloom:
If live the abodes unvexed and balmy—
No equinox with annual doom;
If Eden's wafted from the plume
Of shining Raphael, Michael palmy;
If these in more than fable be,
With natures variously divine—
Through all their ranks they are masculine;
Else how the power with purity?
Or in yon worlds of light is known
The clear intelligence alone?
Express the Founder's words declare,
Marrying none is in the heaven;
Yet love in heaven itself to spare
Love feminine! Can Eve be riven
From sex, and disengaged retain
Its charm? Think this—then may ye feign
The perfumed rose shall keep its bloom,
Cut off from sustenance of loam.
But if Eve's charm be not supernal,
Enduring not divine transplanting—
Love kindled thence, is that eternal?
Here, here's the hollow—here the haunting!
Ah, love, ah wherefore thus unsure?
Linked art thou—locked, with Self impure?
Yearnings benign the angels know,
Saint Francis and Saint John have felt:
Good-will—desires that overflow,
And reaching far as life is dealt.
That other love!—Oh heavy load—
Is naught then trustworthy but God?

On more hereof, derived in frame
From the eremite's Thebaean flame,
Mused Clarel, taking self to task,
Nor might determined thought reclaim:
But, the waste invoking, this did ask:

"Truth, truth cherubic! claim'st thou worth
Foreign to time and hearts which dwell
Helots of habit old as earth
Suspended 'twixt the heaven and hell?"
But turn thee, rest the burden there;
To-morrow new deserts must thou share.

Canto XXXII - Empty Stirrups

The gray of dawn. A tremor slight:
The trouble of imperfect light
Anew begins. In floating cloud
Midway suspended down the gorge,
A long mist trails white shreds of shroud
How languorous toward the Dead Sea's verge.
Riders in seat halt by the gate:
Why not set forth? For one they wait
Whose stirrups empty be—the Swede.
Still absent from the frater-hall
Since afternoon and vesper-call,
He, they imagined, had but sought
Some cave in keeping with his thought,
And reappear would with the light
Suddenly as the Gileadite
In Obadiah's way. But—no,
He cometh not when they would go.
Dismounting, they make search in vain
Till Clarel—minding him again
Of something settled in his air—
A quietude beyond mere calm—
Whell seen from ledge beside the Palm
Reclined in nook of Bethel stair,
Thitherward led them in a thrill
Of nervous apprehension, till
Startled he stops, with eyes avert
And indicating hand.—
'Tis he—
So undisturbed, supine, inert—
The filmed orbs fixed upon the Tree—
Night's dews upon his eyelids be.
To test if breath remain, none tries:
On those thin lips a feather lies—
An eagle's, wafted from the skies.
The vow: and had the genius heard,
Benignant? nor had made delay,
But, more than taking him at word,

Quick wafted where the palm-boughs sway
In Saint John's heaven? Some divined
That long had he been undermined
In frame; the brain a tocsin-bell
Overburdensome for citadel
Whose base was shattered. They refrain
From aught but that dumb look that fell
Identifying; feeling pain
That such a heart could beat, and will—
Aspire, yearn, suffer, baffled still,
And end. With monks which round them stood
Concerned, not discomposed in mood,
Interment they provided for—
Heaved a last sigh, nor tarried more.

Nay; one a little lingered there;
'Twas Rolfe. And as the rising sun,
Though viewless yet from Bethel stair,
More lit the mountains, he was won
To invocation, scarce to prayer:
"Holy Morning,
What blessed lore reservest thou,
Withheld from man, that evermore
Without surprise,
But, rather, with a hurtless scorning
In thy placid eyes,
Thou viewest all events alike?
Oh, tell me, do thy bright beams strike
The healing hills of Gilead now?"

And glanced toward the pale one near
In shadow of the crag's dark brow.—
Did Charity follow that poor bier?
It did; but Bigotry did steer:
Friars buried him without the walls
(Nor in a consecrated bed)
Where vulture unto vulture calls,
And only ill things find a friend:
There let the beak and claw contend
There the hyena's cub be fed:
Heaven that disclaims, and him beweeps
In annual showers; and the tried spirit sleeps.

END OF THIRD PART

Herman Melville was born in New York City on August 1st, 1819, the third of eight children.

At the age of 7 Melville contracted scarlet fever which was to permanently diminish his eyesight. At this time Melville was described as being "very backwards in speech and somewhat slow in comprehension."

Melville attended the Albany Academy from October 1830 to October 1831, where he took the standard preparatory course; reading and spelling; penmanship; arithmetic; English grammar; geography; natural history; universal, Greek, Roman and English history; classical biography; and Jewish antiquities.

The reasons for Melville leaving the Academy after a year are unknown although his brothers continued their education there for a few more months.

In December, Melville's father returned from New York City by steamboat, but difficult weather forced him to travel the last 70 miles in an open carriage in freezing temperatures. A cold developed into delirium and by January 28th, not yet fifty, his father was dead. Melville, at home by now, most probably witnessed much of this event and two decades later he described scenes that must have been very similar in the death of Pierre's father in Pierre.

The family were now in very straitened times. Just 14 Melville took a job in a bank paying $150 a year that he obtained via his uncle, Peter Gansevoort, who was one of the directors of the New York State Bank.

Melville was briefly able to attend again the Albany Academy from October 1836 to March 1837, where he studied the classics.

After a failed stint as a surveyor he signed on to go to sea and travelled across the Atlantic to Liverpool and then on further voyages to the Pacific on adventures which would soon become the architecture of his novels. Whilst travelling he joined a mutiny, was jailed, fell in love with a South Pacific beauty and became known as a figure of opposition to the coercion of native Hawaiians to the Christian religion.

He drew from these experiences in his books Typee, Omoo, and White-Jacket. These were published as novels, the first initially in London in 1846.

They sold very well and enabled him to write full time although royalties were not vast. (During his career it is estimated his writing brought him no more than $10,000)

After a three-month courtship of Elizabeth Shaw, daughter of a prominent Boston family, her father was the Chief Justice of the Massachusetts Supreme Judicial Court, they decided to marry. Her father initially turned down Melville's request but on August 14th, 1847 they married. After initially settling in New York they moved to Massachusetts.

In September of 1850, Melville borrowed $3,000 from his father-in-law Lemuel Shaw to buy a 160-acre farm in Pittsfield. Melville christened the new home 'Arrowhead', due to the quantity of arrowheads dug up around the property during planting season.

That winter, Melville on an impulse paid a visit to the writer Nathaniel Hawthorne. At the time Hawthorne was finishing The House of the Seven Gables and "not in the mood for company". Hawthorne's wife Sophia entertained him while he waited for Hawthorne to come down for supper, and gave him copies of Twice-Told Tales and, The Grandfather's Chair. Melville, sensing a friendship developing, invited them to Arrowhead during the coming weeks. When Sophia agreed, he looked forward to "discussing the Universe with a bottle of brandy & cigars" with Hawthorne.

By 1851 his masterpiece, Moby Dick, was ready to be published. It is perhaps, and certainly at the time, one of the most ambitious novels ever written. However, it never sold out its initial print run of 3,000 and Melville's earnings on this masterpiece were a mere $556.37.

In succeeding years his reputation waned and he found life increasingly difficult. His family was growing, now four children, and a stable income was essential.

From 1853 to 1856, Melville began to publish his short stories in the growing magazine market, most notably "Bartleby, the Scrivener" (1853), "The Encantadas" (1854), and "Benito Cereno" (1855). These and others were later collected together and published in 1856 as the Plazza Tales.

In 1857, he travelled to England where, for the first time since 1852, he reunited with Hawthorne. He then went on to tour the Near East. The Confidence-Man was the last prose work that he published that same year. It received little attention.

With his finances in a disappointing state Melville took the advice of friends that a change in career was called for. For many others public lecturing had proved very rewarding. From late 1857 to 1860, Melville embarked upon three lecture tours, where he spoke mainly on Roman statuary and sightseeing in Rome. These lectures mocked the pseudo-intellectualism of lyceum culture. His words though were ignored by contemporary audiences.

In the 1860's he wrote many poems, many based on the Civil War. But there was no publisher for him and no audience.

In 1866, Melville's wife and her relatives used their influence to obtain a position for him as customs inspector for the City of New York, With his writings almost ignored they moved to New York where Melville joined the New York Customs house and worked there for the next 19 years.

For Melville his early promise and great talents seemed to be getting him nowhere in literary terms. Despite periods of drinking, depression and other ails Elizabeth stood by her husband despite calls from other family members and the marriage held together.

In 1876 he was at last able to publish privately his 16,000 line epic poem Clarel, in which a young American student of divinity travels to Jerusalem to renew his faith. It was to no avail. The book had an initial printing of 350 copies, but sales failed miserably, and the unsold copies were burned when Melville was unable to afford to buy them at cost.

On December 31st, 1885 Melville was at last able to retire. His wife had inherited several small legacies and with her astute ways it was enough to provide them with a reasonable income and Melville had enough to buy further precious books and supplies.

In these last few years Melville finished two poetry collections which were printed privately, although only 25 copies of each; John Marr and Other Sailors (1888) and Timoleon (1891).

Herman Melville, novelist, poet, short story writer and essayist, died at his home on September 28rh 1891 from cardiovascular disease.

He was interred in the Woodlawn Cemetery in The Bronx, New York City.

He was the first writer to have his works collected and published by the Library of America.

Herman Melville – A Concise Bibliography

Novels, Short Stories & Poetry

Typee: A Peep at Polynesian Life (1846)
Omoo: A Narrative of Adventures in the South Seas (1847)
Mardi: And a Voyage Thither (1849)
Redburn: His First Voyage (1849)
White-Jacket; or, The World in a Man-of-War (1850)
Moby-Dick; or, The Whale (1851)
Pierre: or, The Ambiguities (1852)
Isle of the Cross (1853 unpublished, and now lost)
Cock-A-doodle-Doo (Short story) (1852)
Bartleby, the Scrivener (Short story) (1853)
The Encantadas, or Enchanted Isles (Short story) (1854)
Poor Man's Pudding and Rich Man's Crumbs (Short story) (1854)
The Happy Failure (Short story) (1854)
The Lightning-Rod Man (Short story) (1854)
The Fiddler (Short story) (1854)
Benito Cereno (1855)
Israel Potter: His Fifty Years of Exile (1855)
The Paradise of Batchelors and the Tartarus of Maids (Short story) (1855)
The Bell-Tower (Short story) (1855)
Jimmy Rose (Short story) (1855)
The Gees (Short story) (1856)
I and My Chimney (Short story) (1856)
The Apple-Tree Story (Short story) (1856)
The Confidence-Man: His Masquerade (1857)
The Piazza (Short story) (1856)
Battle-Pieces and Aspects of the War (Poetry) (1866)
Clarel: A Poem and Pilgrimage in the Holy Land (Epic poem) (1876)
John Marr and Other Sailors (Poetry) (1888)
Timoleon (Poetry) (1891)
Billy Budd, Sailor (An Inside Narrative) (1891 unfinished, published posthumously in 1924)